Rural Organization
in Bukoba District, Tanzania

Jørgen and Karen Rald

Rural Organization in Bukoba District, Tanzania

The Scandinavian Institute of African Studies
Uppsala 1975

© 1975 Jørgen and Karen Rald and Nordiska afrikainstitutet

ISBN 91-7106-082-0

Printed in Sweden by

Almqvist & Wiksell Tryckeri AB, Uppsala 1975

Contents

Acknowledgements

This study is based on research done in Tanzania from January 1968 to July 1971. Nearly two and a half years were spent in the field in Bukoba District. One of the authors was a Research Fellow in the Bureau of Resource Assessment and Land Use Planning (BRALUP), University of Dar es Salaam, the post being granted by the Danish International Development Agency (DANIDA).

The research was supervised by the three successive directors of BRALUP, Bob Kates, Len Berry and Adolpho Mascarenhas, for whose encouragement and assistance we are most grateful.

The Evangelical Lutheran Church of Western Tanzania placed a missionary house in Rwantege at our disposal during our field work. The Church also took great interest in our work and assisted us with discussions and comments. We particularly wish to thank Bishop J. Kibira, and we very much remember the good neighbourliness of Sister Anna Borg.

It is impossible to thank all the people in the Regional and the District administrations at Farmers' Training Centres and in the Bukoba Cooperative Union. We thus record our indebtedness to the former Regional Commissioner of West Lake, Sam Simon Shemsanga, who not only supported us officially but also took deep personal interest in the work. It is difficult to find the appropriate words to thank all the Bahaya we have met. Without their cooperation, hospitality, warmness and open attitude to foreigners, we would not have been able to carry out our work. A more profound feeling emerged during the field work, a sense of being so much at home that we felt Tanzania, and especially Buhaya, to be our adopted country. We are indebted to various university students for their assistance in data processing, and also to the young farmers in the Nshamba area who worked for us as assistants or enumerators. Our special thanks also go to our first assistant Jackson Kishumo, who took over the full responsibility for the time study in the last five months.

To record our deep gratitude to the Bahaya, we have dedicated this book to ''our old father'' Belenado Bakula Lushanshumwa, of Bugombe in Kanyigo.

For reading and giving valuable criticism of the manuscript we offer our sincere thanks to A. A. Moody, S. Mutasa and B. Mbakileki.

The photos are by J. Kirknes, except page 61 and page 112 by J. Rald.

The manuscript was finished 1972.

Hvidbjerg, Skive, June 1975

Jørgen and Karen Rald

Preface

This is a book about people living in the rural areas in Bukoba District, Tanzania. They all cultivate land for the production of food and cash crops, but they are also engaged in other economic activities. Although in the first half of the book we have put emphasis on land use, land tenure and agricultural extension, this is not a specific study of farmers but a study of how people in Bukoba (the Bahaya) organize their life in society with regard to space and time.

The second half of the book deals with the allocation of time and labour, and income expenditure for selected households in Nshamba ward. The study was carried out between 1968 and 1971, that is, in the early days of the policy of *ujamaa* in Tanzania. We end the book with an outline of the social and political aspects of the farming system.

Methods of Investigation

We started our study with a geographical approach. Land-use mapping was the basic technique used as an entry to the analysis of the rural organization. Detailed farm-unit land-use maps provided an essential area reference for the study of the productivity and land-tenure problems. The land-use maps formed the basis for the investigation of the allocation of family labour and employed labourers; they were also important for the understanding of the division of work between men and women. Furthermore, the land-use maps exposed changes in cultivation techniques and thereby the results of extension service.

Mapping of farm units also revealed that the rural population could not be treated as a homogeneous group. The diversity in the appearance of physical units during the mapping process disclosed a rural society with a very wide range in standards of living and ways of life, varying from pure subsistence farming to a mixed economy of farming and wage-earning. The individual households also cultivated areas ranging very widely in size, and the composition of their labour force was highly varied.

The first step of the data collection, i.e., the mapping, worked successfully. The second step of the survey was an attempt to obtain adequate single-interview information on socio-economic aspects of the farming system and the rural society, in order to minimize cost and effort. This part of the survey proved unsuccessful. Detailed and *reliable* data on labour input, yields and household expenditure could not be obtained from a single interview.

The third step consisted of a very detailed recording of selected households concerning allocation of time, labour and capital. Yields were measured and land tenure problems investigated. We paid a great deal of attention to the policy of agricultural extension in Bukoba, but we grew ever more convinced of the importance of understanding the social and political role of land, crops and cattle in relation to the specific Haya traditions, and in relation to the Tanzanian policy of socialism and rural development.

Farmers or peasants?

Throughout the book we use the term 'farmer'. The population of the rural society has been divided into two groups in the time-study sample; full-time farmers and part-time farmers. We found these categories applicable according to the economic and social structure of the households and their mode of production, even if we have from time to time used the terms 'peasant economy' and 'peasant society'.

Although scholars have shown an increasing interest in the study of peasant societies, it has been difficult to apply their various definitions of peasantry to the Bukoba population as such.

Shanin (1971) defines peasantry analytically: "The peasantry consists of small agricultural producers who, with the help of simple equipment and the labour of their families, produce mainly for their own consumption and for the fulfilment of obligations to the holders of political and economic power." This could partly apply to that group of the Bukoba population which was under *nyarubanja* before Independence.

Chayanov's (1966) theory of peasant economy, however, with its built-in labour-consumer balance, could provide a good fit for some of the poorer Bahaya households today.

Due to the capitalistic framework and the stratification of the Haya society, we use the term 'farmers'; nevertheless, we avoid the term 'farm' for a farm-unit area of, e.g., 0.94 ha. As a gesture of compromise, we use the term 'farmer' to refer to people engaged in agricultural activities, including food crops, cash crops and livestock, dependent upon family labour and hired labour and with access to income from non-agricultural sectors.

The term 'farmer' has also been criticized from a political point of view: "A peasant economy cannot harbour farmers. The few present are simply kulaks" (Mbakileki 1973). We agree with that when seen in the context of Tanzania as a whole but we nevertheless found the term 'peasant' not satisfactory for describing the economic conditions of Bukoba society in 1968–1970. The colonial programme of growing coffee and the educational facilities available in the district had a great influence on the development of the socio-economic structure of Bukoba society up to 1967.

Chapter 1. The Physical Features and Resources of Buhaya

Topography

The district consists of a series of mountain ridges running from north to south, parallel to the shore of Lake Victoria. The first mountain ridge forms the Bumbire Islands, 16 km to the east of the Lake shore. The second forms the lake shore ridge or escarpment of an altitude of about 1 200 m above sea level (the mean Lake level is 1 125 m). Between the second and the third ridge (the Gera-Kamachumu Biirabo ridge, which reaches an altitude of 1 560 m), the Ngono river and its tributaries form a valley and a drainage system.

The ridges terminate in rugged scarps breaking off in bold sandstone cliffs. The summits of the ridges are relatively flat and vary in extent from 1 km to 20 km. The broad-topped ridges have been designated as plateaus and the narrow ones ridges.

The flattish summits are apparently a part of an old erosion surface (Milne 1938). Gradually this old surface was heaved up and tilted. Fault scarps were formed, water carved new valleys, and the old surface was cut into plateaus and ridges. As tilting continued, the topography at many places took the form of cuesta landscapes and checked the flow of the north-running streams, creating extensive swamp areas between the ridges—especially to the north, at the outlets of the rivers. (See profile sections, p. 30.)

Water and gravity continued to work on the landscape. The broad summits today provide extensive areas of rolling hills, intersected by small V-shaped valleys. The hill slopes are another distinguishing feature of the topography: the upper slopes are steep, while the middle and lower slopes have a gentle gradient.

Numerous small streams running from east to west (down to the main rivers) cut back into the plateaus and ridges, increasing the intersection of the landscape and at places forming peninsulas of usable land in the swamps.

Geology and soils[1]

Bukoba District is nearly entirely dominated by Bukoba sandstone, which is the parent rock. Bukoba sandstone consists mainly of compact fine and medium-grained sandstone, in which are interbedded shale-like rocks consisting of a fine aggregate of quartz and sericite (a form of mica). This sandy shale is at several places exposed at the surface; the thickness of these strata is clearly evident when roads are cut through anticlinals.[2] The coarser sandstone consists of practically nothing but quartz grains and cementing silica. The fine-grained shale-like sandstones contain, besides quartz, a clay-forming mineral in considerable quantity. Thus the two kinds of sandstones provide a range of soils from pure sands to loamy sands, or sandy clay.

Each rock gives rise to a wide range of locally derived soils; because of the topography, however, all have more or less contributed, through transported debris, to the mixed cover of the slopes. Møberg (1970) has observed that in general the ferralsols[3] dominate the hills and slopes where the Bukoban sandstone is the parent rock. In the same area one normally finds lacustrine deposits, fluvisols, gleisols and in a few cases vertisols in the flat parts of the valleys.

The dominating ferralsols vary in colour from dark reddish-brown and dark yellowish-brown in high-rainfall areas near the Lake shore to more yellowish-red and red colour in rainfall-poor areas—towards the west and south of the Lake. The texture in the rather uniform profile often changes from a sandy topsoil to a subsoil with increasingly clayey texture.

Laterization

The present minerals have long been under the influence of chemical decomposition. The decomposition has been accelerated by the tropical climate: moderate warmth and heavy leaching due to the high rainfall. Under these conditions there has been a tendency towards laterization. From different soil surveys it can be seen that iron concretions in the soils can be found all over the slopes, but are not necessarily present in large amounts, as the soil can be situated directly on the parent material. The iron concretions vary from a loose

Diagram 1

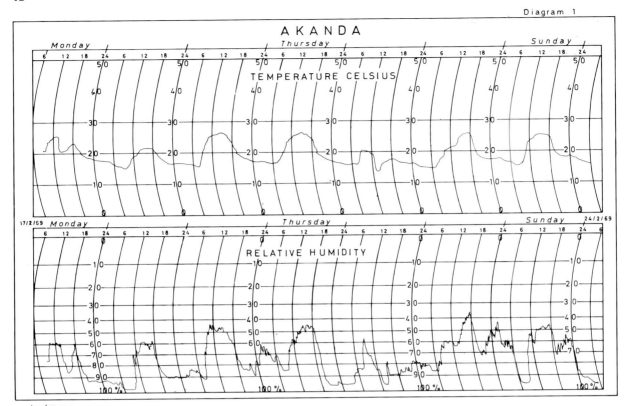

kr/mmm

Diagram 2

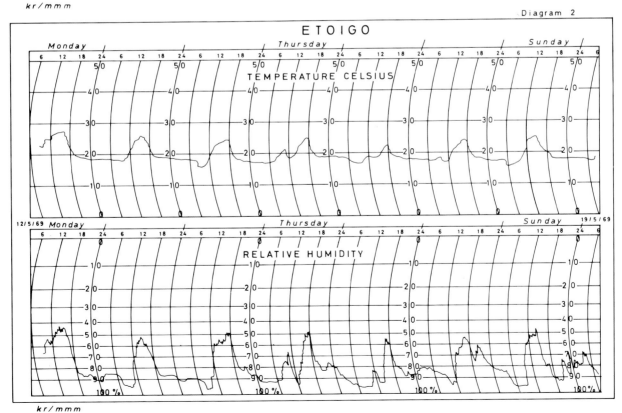

kr/mmm

Diagram 3

EKYANDA

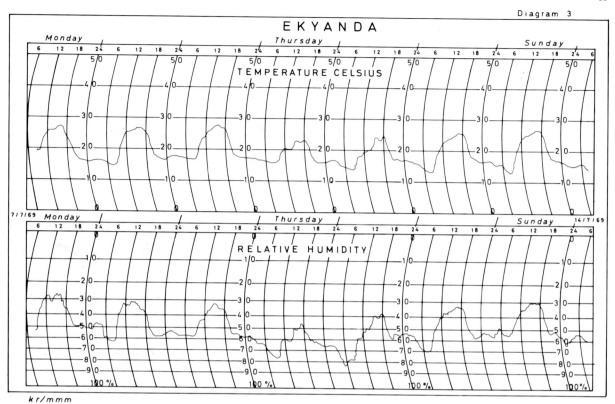

kr/mmm

Diagram 4

OMUHANGUKO

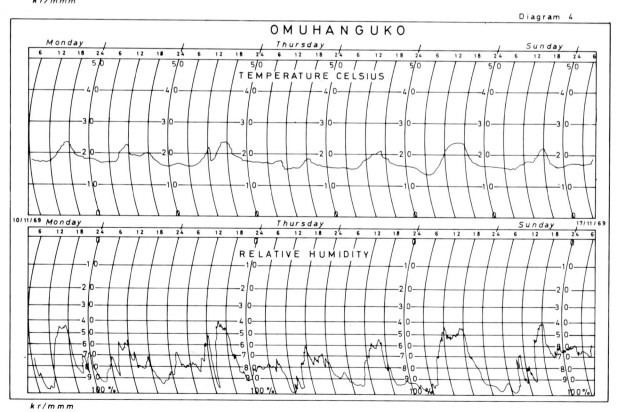

kr/mmm

14

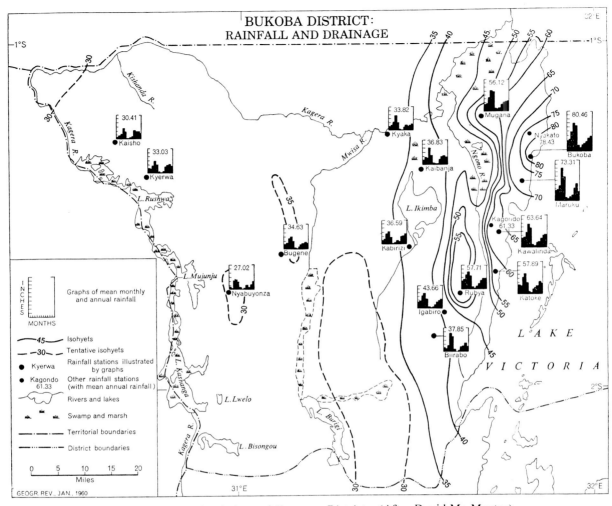

Map 1. *Rainfall and hydrography of Bukoba and Karagwe Districts.* (After David Me Muster)

'murram', sometimes of considerable depth, to a real hardpan of laterite.

Due to the action of erosion, the topsoil and subsoil have been washed away on the upper parts of the slopes, so that the vegetation grows directly on the iron concretions, the 'murram' soil.

Soils in low-lying flat areas

The soils in the low-lying flat areas of the broad swampy valley bottom or in bays with lacustrine deposits differ from the ferralsols in that they have either a high content of montmorillonite clay minerals or are made up of pure sandy deposits.

Soil depth

The variety of soils in the area is important for the understanding of the land-use pattern, but it may well be the case that the soil-depth variation is a far more important localization factor for the present land use.

According to the topography of the area, the depth of the soil profile varies considerably. On the level plateau tops the soil is generally more than two metres deep, without any iron concretions. On the slopes the soil depth varies according to the convex or concave shape of the slope (Prynø 1970). On the convex slope the deepest soil is found on the upper and lower parts of the slope, and on the concave slope the soil depth increases from the middle of the slope downwards.

There is a correlation between the gradient of the slope and the variation in the depth of the soil.

The depth in question is the soil profile down to the layer of iron concretions, the A horizon. It must be borne in mind that on many slopes the B horizon can consist of a loose 'murram' layer of considerable depth, and with potential value for agricultural use. Finally, it should be mentioned that there exists a relationship between the amount of rainfall and the minimum soil depth for the crops grown in Bukoba District.

Water table and moisture content

Connected with the depth of the soil profile down to a layer which is impenetrable for the roots of the vegetation is the depth of the fluctuating water table. The water table fluctuates according to the seasonal variation in rainfall. A high water table can have a negative influence on certain main crops such as bananas and coffee.

There are different opinions about the water-holding capacity of the ferralsol soils. Generally it has been stated that these soils have an extremely low water-holding capacity, but recent observations (Rald 1968 and Møberg 1970) show that "even in the last part of the dry season, the quite sandy ferralsol soils had a relative high content of moisture once one reached the depth of 50–60 cm or more below the soil surface" (Møberg 1970).

Climate

Temperature

Situated between latitude 1°00′ S and 2°15′ S, Bukoba District has an equatorial climate. There is not much variation in the monthly mean temperature throughout the year: it remains about 20°C. The daily temperature fluctuates between a daily mean minimum of 15°C and a daily mean maximum of 25°C, with a margin of ±4°C.

The four diagrams with temperature and relative humidity show characteristic examples from the four Haya seasons. (See pages 12–13.) Diagram 3, *Ekyanda*, shows the season the Haya people call the cool and dry season, and the diagram illustrates how the daily temperature fluctuations are wider and the humidity lower than in the other seasons. Otherwise, the uniform pattern of the equatorial climate is striking.

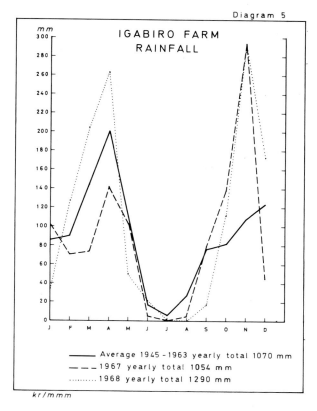

Diagram 5

IGABIRO FARM RAINFALL

——— Average 1945 - 1963 yearly total 1070 mm
— — — 1967 yearly total 1054 mm
.... 1968 yearly total 1290 mm

kr/mmm

Rainfall

For an area with a marked relief, as in Bukoba District with its north-south running mountain ridges, one can expect the factors causing spatial variations to be related to the relief pattern. Looking at the rainfall map[4] and the yearly average figures for the stations located on the map, there seems to be an interrelation between the atmospheric processes, relief and distance from the Lake shore. This interaction in the Bukoba area, however, is quite complicated, as the atmospheric processes causing precipitation are not only due to the seasonal wind reversal with the passing of the intertropical convergence zone, but from time to time also to Atlantic air, which can reach as far as Bukoba District through the Congo basin.

In the Lake littoral zone of Bukoba District about 12 rain gauge stations are working (but only two fully equipped meteorological stations). Three of the 12 stations have average records for more than the past 30 years. The remaining stations have average records for 15 years.

The rainfall map must be read with caution; it merely gives the general trends for long-term periods. The

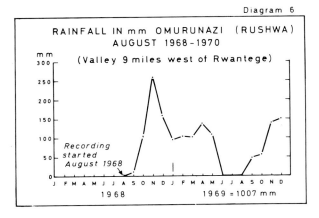

Diagram 6

RAINFALL IN mm OMURUNAZI (RUSHWA)
AUGUST 1968 - 1970

(Valley 9 miles west of Rwantege)

Recording started August 1968

1968   1969 = 1007 mm

highest rainfall area is in the vicinity of Bukoba town (over 2 000 mm). Interesting to note is the very regular concentric pattern around Bukoba Town. This may perhaps be due to specific topographic features or due to the directions of the trades, in that the town is located nearly half-way along the western Lake shore. It may also be due to the fact that the rain gauge at the airstrip is located at Lake level. The Bukoba Town rain gauge is the one furthest to the north along the Lake shore and the only one at lake level. All other stations are placed at the top of the Lake shore ridge.

Towards the south, along the Lake shore, rainfall decreases: to 994 mm at Karambi and down to 753 mm at Nyamirembe. Towards the west we see the same trend but the steepness of the gradient varies with the topography. Where the lower inland is near the shore, as in Ibwera area, the gradient from east to west is rather steep, but passing the Kamachumu–Biirabo plateau the gradient is more gentle. In the broad basin between Bukoba ridges and the ridges in Karagwe, the rainfall drops to an estimated amount of 762 mm, and then increases on the Karagwe mountain slopes to 1 200 mm.

The same southward tendency as noted for the Lake shore can be recognized for the plateau areas.

Yearly distribution of rainfall

The rainfall diagrams show that for all areas the same distribution pattern is found. The rainfall is rather well distributed over the year. The wet season has two peaks, a major one between March and May and a minor one between November and December. The dry season lasts only three months, from June to September with July as the really dry month. Even in these months the northern part of the District receives

some precipitation, whereas to the south July and August can be completely dry.

Diagram 5, from Igabiro Farmers' Training Centre, situated 3 miles south of Rwantege, gives the average rainfall (for 18 years) for the southern part of the plateau. Compared with Diagrams 6 and 7, Diagram 5 is a good example of how average figures hide fluctuations from year to year.

As the Rwantege figures (Diagram 7) indicate, there is considerable variation from year to year, both in quantity and distribution. In the peak month, March, Rwantege received only 69 mm in 1969 as opposed to 204 mm in 1968, and the important month, September (the beginning of the agricultural year) received only 17 mm in 1968.

Much of the precipitation falls as thunderstorms (mainly in the morning hours), and in this area the interrelation between atmospheric processes and the relief gives rise to very extreme local precipitation, with considerable rainfall gradients over very short distances.

This is illustrated by the monthly rainfall figures for two stations located at 5 km from each other. Omurunazi (altitude 4 200 feet) is in a valley below the plateau to the west. Rwantege (altitude 5 000 feet) is on the western top of the plateau. (See Diagrams 6 and 7.)

Thus the station in the valley, expected to be in a rain shadow position when related to the plateau, received 119 mm more than the station at the top of the plateau. (The two gauges were set up and checked by the author.)

Looking at Diagram 8, which shows daily periods, the local character of rainfall distribution is even more striking. It seems that over a short period of time the atmospheric processes play a dominant role, while the

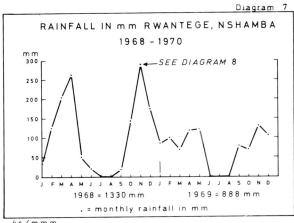

Diagram 7

RAINFALL IN mm RWANTEGE, NSHAMBA
1968 - 1970

←SEE DIAGRAM 8

1968 = 1330 mm   1969 = 888 mm

. = monthly rainfall in mm

kr / mmm

interrelation between atmospheric processes, relief and distance from the Lake shore gives the long-term pattern of rainfall distribution in Bukoba District.

Rainfall distribution and agricultural activities

In Chapter 5 the distribution of rainfall over the year and the yearly distribution of labour input in agriculture are related, but one example here will show the importance of the distribution problem.

If we compare the various monthly rainfalls for Rwantege (see Diagram 7) for the month of September, we shall see that the station received 79 mm in 1969 and only 17 mm in 1968. For agricultural work, this meant that people who planted annual crops like beans and maize at the beginning of September 1968 (after the first showers had occurred) had to replant in October because the first crops did not root. In 1969 the planting started in mid-September and succeeded because there was ample rainfall. Likewise, the harvesting of coffee started late in May in 1969 while in 1968 it had started around the first of May in the same area.

The higher rainfall in the northern part of the District allows the farmers to harvest two crops of beans a year, while the farmers in the south harvest only one crop.

Of the 262 mm precipitation in November 1968, 60 mm fell in two hours on the 25th of November. Such heavy rainfall has more erosive effect on the soils than any possible benefits it might have on agriculture.

Of the 173 mm received in December, 52 mm also fell in a few hours' time, in such a heavy storm that hundreds of banana plants were beaten down and big trees blew over, destroying crops and houses. Again,

Table 1. *Days with rainfall. September 1968 and 1969. Rwantege in Nshamba*

1968	mm	1969	mm
4 Sept.	4	4 Sept.	23
20 Sept.	13	6 Sept.	15
		15 Sept.	32
		25 Sept.	6
		30 Sept.	3
Total	17 mm		79 mm

this storm was very local and was not even recorded at the nearby stations of Rubya and Biirabo.

I. Jackson (1969) notes in his paper on rainfall gradients over small areas: "Variations in rainfall of the magnitude indicated for an individual season or year could result in a considerable variation in crop yields over a very small area. This may be particularly relevant to studies of variation in yields and points out the need for a very careful assessment of rainfall over the area considered."

The survey material for physical environment

Bukoba District is one of the few areas in Tanzania covered by excellent 1 : 50 000 scale maps made on the basis of airphoto covers as early as 1961.[5] Thus the researcher is well equipped with very detailed topographic maps with contour lines at 50-foot intervals. The important point here is that because of their excellent signature cover compiled from the airphotos, these map sheets provide general land-use maps of the District, revealing in detail such land-use features as: forest, thicket, woodland, scrub, scattered trees, palms, mangrove swamp, papyrus swamp, marsh, seasonal swamp. The maps also show with great accuracy the location of perennial crops, mainly coffee and bananas, in the year 1961.

Notes

1. The main soil surveys done in the area are:
Milne (1938), Agricultural officer West Lake (1955), Sir A. Gibbs (1956), Rald (1968), *Soil Survey Unit-Ukiriguru* (1969), Møberg (1970) and Prynø (1971). The present description is a compilation from these authors' works.

2. Anticlinal: when strata dip like the roof of a house.

3. Ferralsols: soils having a high content of free sesquioxides of iron and/or aluminium, and having a relatively high clay content and a relatively low cation exchange capacity.

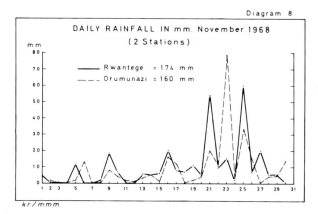

Diagram 8

DAILY RAINFALL IN mm. November 1968 (2 Stations)
Rwantege = 174 mm
Orumunazi = 160 mm

2—752437 Rald

Fluvisols: soils from recent alluvial lacustrine deposits.
Gleisols: soils without horizons other than a mottled gleyic horizon.
Vertisols: widely cracking gray to black soil having a high content of expanding-lattice clay minerals. (After Møberg. 1973)

4. Three rainfall maps with rather different isohyets have been produced from West Lake Region:

i. Gibbs et al. (1956)
ii. David McMaster (1960)
iii. S. B. Jensen (1968)

The present map is reproduced from McMaster with the author's permission.

5. It is interesting to note the extensive use of these maps in dividing the District into 599 small enumeration areas during the 1967 census.

It is equally interesting to note the strange neglect of these maps in everyday activities among planners, development officers and field assistants, except for the Water Development and Irrigation Development Unit (WD & ID) and Comworks.

When an overall planning exercise was carried out in 1967 for a development plan for the Regions, these maps were not used, and acreage of potential land was merely estimated.

When 20 new settlements were established in 1968 in the region, the sites for these villages were found with the aid of local people, which in some cases led to serious mislocations. Later on, the Land Planning Officers used a great amount of time to demarcate the boundaries of the settlement areas, using chains and compasses in traversing the areas—a job which could have been done in one week on an enlarged section of the 1 : 50 000 map with field checking.

These maps seem not to have been supplied to the districts. The maps ought to be supplied as standard equipment for every field assistant. This supply should be followed up by intensive training in map interpretation and measurement conversion.

Officials are still using old and out-of-date district maps. The Agricultural Officers and Field Assistant Officers (Bwana Shambas), who often know their areas very well, could make intensive use of these maps.

The Water Division could speed up work and assist all departments in the Region if equipped with adequate machinery for enlargement and reduction of maps.

Chapter 2. Land Use

Dividing Bukoba District into rough categories, L. and E. Berry (1969) found the following distribution of land uses.

Table 2. *Land Use in Bukoba District*

	ha	Per cent of total area
Smallholder cultivation	120 000	15.1
Rough grazing land	597 975	75.3
Estates	2 500	0.3
High altitude forest	12 500	1.6
Other woods forest	20 000	2.5
Other: urban, rocky, swamps	40 625	5.1
Total	793 600	99.9

The land use of the district clearly shows a marked line for cultivation towards the west, coinciding with the isohyet 875 mm and the longitude 21°27′ E.

West of this line the District is completely empty with regard to settlements and cultivation. This applies to the basin between Bukoba ridges and the Karagwe Highland, and to the triangle plain towards the northwest, north of the Kagera River.

The cultivated area with smallholder settlements is thus concentrated in the Lake littoral zone with a maximum width of 45 km to the north and 30 km to the south. With the present technological level and the present price level on agricultural output, this is the potential zone for the Bahaya farmers.

A part of this zone is shown on the topographic land-use map (Map No. 2), with its island pattern of *kibanja* land, where dots indicate smallholder settlements with coffee and banana cultivation; the white areas in between are Rweya land.

We shall now apply the same categories of land use for this potential zone, upon which the picture changes radically.

The grazing land is not only used for grazing the rather small population of cattle but is also used for cultivating the annual crops: groundnuts, bambarra nuts, yams, millet, etc. The crucial point at present is

Table 3. *Land Use for Lake Littoral Zone 1969*

	ha	Per cent of total area
Smallholder cultivation	120 000	45.4
Rough grazing land	68 375	25.9
Estates	2 500	0.9
Forest, wooded area	32 500	12.4
Other: urban, rocky, swamps	40 625	15.4
Total	264 000	100.0

that these crops are cultivated in a shifting cultivation system, i.e., a plot is cultivated for one year or one year and a half, and then is left fallow to regain its fertility under grass for a period of 6–8 years. This implies that to cultivate one hectare with annual crops the farmers need 8 hectares of grassland. About 75 per cent of the smallholders cultivate annual crops on the grassland.

Travelling through the District early in the morning or late in the afternoon, when the sun is low and casts long shadows, it is striking to see the configuration of the annual-crops cultivation pattern on the slopes. The elongated mounds up and down the slopes covered with grass fallow cause the slopes to look like corrugated iron. From the north to just south of Mubunda every piece of usable land is either under cultivation or lies fallow (see photo page 23).

North of the Bukoba–Kyaka road (in Bugabo and Kyamutwara divisions of Kiziba) the topography—with its narrow ridges and extensive swampland—leaves no room at all for the expansion of cultivation for the very dense population. The range is from 50 to 100 persons per square kilometre. Farmers nevertheless put new land under cultivation in the marginal areas along the swamps, but a major feature for these northern areas is the migration towards the west and the south.[1]

Migration

The migration trend mentioned above applies to the district down to the Mubunda area. People from the northern divisions and from around Bukoba town and the Maruku area have migrated to the area near Lake Ikimba, whereas people from the large plateau have moved to the west below the escarpment and further out beyond the last north–south running ridge. There is a long line of first-generation villages trying to push cultivation out in the marginal lowland area in the eastern part of the great basin.

People from the southern part of the plateau move both south and west, but at the same time other tribes like the Zinza, the Ha and the Subi have moved from Ngara district into this southern area. People from Rwanda and Burundi have traditionally taken up work in Bukoba as casual labourers and some of these people have in recent years settled as farmers. They have either opened up new land or settled in *ujamaa* villages.

For the Lake littoral zone there is already a shortage of land, and with the present land use and cultivation system this shortage will have reached a critical stage by the end of the century.

The functional content of the main land-use types

The Haya farmers divide their land use into different functional land-use types. Here a land-use type is defined as not only the actual cover of land with vegetation, but the functional use of land and the social values attached to the different land-use types. It has been found convenient to apply the Haya terms to the land-use types:[2] (1) *Kibanja*, (2) *Ekishambu*, (3) *Orweya* and (4) *omusiri*.

1. *Kibanja—Bananas. Kibanja* (plural *bibanja*) is the name given to a plot of land cultivated with the perennial crops banana and coffee.[3] Throughout Buhaya, people distinguish by name between 183 different types of bananas for cooking and for making beer. The names do not cover different species or varieties but mainly sub-species deriving from two wild species, *Musa acuminata* and *Musa balbasiana*. The majority of edible bananas deriving from the above-mentioned species are classified under the name *Eumusa*. The 183 collected names (Maruku 1968) often cover the same sub-species within different areas, as the bananas are locally classified according to the appearance and form of the fruit, and the taste when cooked or processed.

There are four main varieties of bananas. *Ebitoke* is the common name for the cooking bananas[4] which are the dominant group of sub-species cultivated in the

kibanja. They form the staple food in the whole area and are normally harvested shortly before they ripen. They are peeled and cooked before they are eaten. The Bahaya are so devoted to bananas that they will eat cooking bananas 365 days a year if possible.

Embire is the common name for the sub-species used for making beer.

The bananas are harvested shortly before they are ripe, and the beer-making process is often as follows:

1. A large hole is dug in the ground.
2. Dry banana leaves mixed with fresh leaves are used to line the hole.
3. The unripened banana bunches are heaped in the hole, with glowing charcoal wrapped in dry grass put in between the bunches.
4. The bunches are covered with fresh banana leaves and soil, leaving a small hole on one side to serve as an inlet.
5. For three days smoke is led in to the bananas through the small hole.
6. On the fourth day the soil cover is removed but the banana bunches remain covered by the fresh leaves.
7. On the sixth day the bananas are ripe and are taken out of the hole for *pombe* making.
8. Then the ripe bananas are put into a big canoelike container carved out of a tree trunk. The bananas can be peeled before being put into the container; then the juice made is called *entondole* in Kihaya. If the bananas are put into the boat unpeeled, the juice produced is called *ebishushu*.
9. The bananas are then mixed with certain types of grass, particularly two species, *eshoju*, i.e., *imperata* and *eyojwe*, i.e., *Loudetia Kageransis* or *Simplex*, which do not produce scent.

The brewers walk to and fro in the container, squeezing the juice out of the bananas with their feet. Only the men are allowed to use this technique. When some juice has been collected, women are allowed to participate, squeezing the juice out with their hands into big pots.

10. After the squeezing the container is cleaned; the juice is mixed with water and filtered by passing it through a clean grass sieve. Then sorghum is roasted on a pan and mixed with the juice to help in the fermentation process.
11. The container, with the brew in it, is covered with fresh banana leaves which are tied tightly around it. The brew is then left to ferment for a period varying from one to several days.

Friedrich (1968) estimates that approximately one-

21

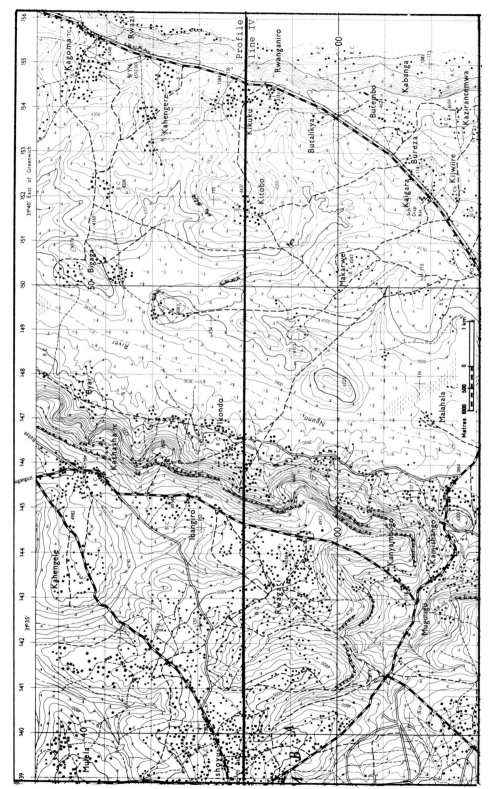

Map 2. *Topographic land-use.* Detail from Map Sheet 913, Series 4742, 1 : 50 000.

22

The Ndolage escarpment seen from the East. On the top of the plateau villages with big trees for fuel. Under the escarpment villages intermixed with Rweya land. In the foreground one woman and two girls are carrying grass bundles to the village.

third of the bananas grown in his sample area were used for beer brewing. This seems a fairly reliable figure, as farmers who for religious reasons do not drink beer themselves normally nevertheless cultivate the bananas used to make beer, either as a cash crop or for contributions to relatives or friends.

Nkonjwa is the name for the species used for roasting. They are mainly served as a delicacy for guests. *Ebiise* is the name given to the above-mentioned species when they are eaten ripe and fresh as a sweet. This is done mainly by children and by old people when they are travelling. (In Kiziba called *ebyenju*.)

In general bananas grow well in a climate with an annual rainfall of 1 250 mm (50 inches), but more important is the fact that 50 mm per month "represents a level below which bananas are seriously short of wa-

ter" (Simmonds 1959). In the Lake littoral zone near Bukoba Town this occurs only in the month of July. Moving to the west and south the number of months with rainfall less than 50 mm increases to three: June, July and August (and sometimes September, as well). These months do not cause severe constraints on banana cultivation, but give rise to periodicity in yields over the year. Thus after a prolonged dry season a shortage of bananas will be felt. The Bahaya then begin to talk about 'famine', which means that they must rely on other starchy crops such as sweet potatoes, yams and cassava for some time.

The critical minimum mean temperature is generally considered to be 15°C, which agrees well with a daily mean temperature fluctuating around 15°C. Thus the banana-growing areas in Bukoba District, lying to the

Rweya slope. The patterns of Omusiri cultivation here lying under grass fallow show how every piece of usable land is part of the farming system.

north and east near the Lake shore, have satisfactory climatic conditions, while climatic constraints increase towards the west and south.

Friedrich (1968) underlines that "the considerable variation in the density of growth within the Bukoba District is determined chiefly by annual rainfall. In areas with 35 inches (889 mm) of rain, 650 clumps per acre were counted, as against over 1 100 clumps where rainfalls of 45 inches (1 143 mm) are to be expected."

In Nshamba, an area on the southern part of the large plateau and with a mean annual rainfall of 1 130 mm, the authors found a density ranging from 400 to 800 clumps per acre. The sample plots were all interplanted with coffee, which highly influences the density of the bananas.

For the cultivation of bananas two soil factors are important: *structure* and *depth*. The structure of the soil determines its drainage, which is essential for banana cultivation. A wide range of different soil types can support bananas if they have a good internal drainage, but compact clays and fine sands and silts are bad soils for bananas.

Simmonds (1959) writes, "There is no such thing as a *good banana soil*." To adopt a more pragmatic approach to the question, it is better to ask, "Can this soil be made to grow bananas?" rather than, "Is this a good banana soil?" This is more relevant for an understanding of the location of banana cultivation in the poor soils of Bukoba District. Møberg (1970) notes that "The depth of the soil is of utmost importance, when the question is about cultivation of perennial crops such as plantains, bananas, coffee and tea. Only in high rainfall areas just around Bukoba (town) can a soil having a depth of less than 150 cm either to compact iron concretions, plinthite or other forms of hard-pan, or to parent rock, be used for these crops. In other parts of the Region, the depth of the soil should preferably be more than 180–200 cm for the crops mentioned.'' This is meant to emphasize the importance of the soil's capacity for maintaining a water reserve during the critical last part of the dry season.

Thus the two factors of structure and depth play an equally important role in our understanding of the location pattern, which will be examined in the next chapter.

Kibanja—Coffee. The *kibanja* is also the place for cultivation of the two varieties *Coffee arabica* and *Coffee robusta.* The latter is claimed to be indigenous in African equatorial forests and was the first coffee to be grown on a commercial basis in Bukoba District. At the end of the nineteenth century *Coffee arabica* was introduced by missionaries as a commercial crop.

Both crops were originally interplanted with bananas and have been grown as monoculture (*ukulima wa kisasa*) only within the last decade. Even so, coffee belongs to the land-use type *kibanja.*

Both Robusta coffee and Arabica coffee thrive on a slightly acidic soil, fairly rich in humus and well drained. Both varieties need nearly the same amount of rainfall, about 1 765 mm (75 inches), if the conditions are to be ideal. Robusta grows best in a hot humid climate up to an altitude of 4 500 feet (1 350 m), whereas Arabica thrives better in a cooler climate and is mainly grown from 1 200 to 1 500 m. This means that Robusta coffee dominates the lower ridges in the north and east of the District, while Arabica is predominantly found on the higher plateau. There are, however, numerous overlapping zones, and Robusta is found all over the District because of its role as chewing coffee and in customary ceremonies.

Kibanja—and the village. The term *kibanja* also implies that the plot with perennial crops is inherited or given to the son by his father. In this *kibanja* the son builds a house for his family and a cattle-shed for his few cows; in this house he stores his coffee and other agricultural products. Thus the first *kibanja* is the centre for the nuclear family life and the centre for the management of the farm unit, which consists of several plots of *kibanja* (*bibanja*). The term has an emotional and social implication attached to kinship and descent. The father will usually be buried in his *kibanja;* the eldest son inherits the largest of his father's *kibanja,* including the part where the tomb is situated (see chapter on land tenure).

Often a piece of *kibanja* which is not inherited from the father is called the *shamba* (the Swahili word for a cultivated plot). Even a remote part of the original *kibanja,* primarily cultivated with coffee trees only, can be called a *Shamba.*

It should be mentioned that the perennial crops are interplanted seasonally with beans, maize and pumpkins.

Furthermore, isolated plants of different vegetables find their place in the *kibanja* near the house: tomatoes, pepper, cabbages, sugar canes, yams and fruit trees such as pawpaws, oranges, and mangoes. The *kibanja* is crowded with many crops and each plot is demarcated either by trees of different species, or by a certain plant (*dracaena deremensis Engl.,* of the genus *Agavacea*). In the northern part this plant (see illustration, p. 42) is called *omulamula* (''the one that judges''); and in the southern part of the District it is known as *ekihanyi* (''beacon''). This plant is customarily the *legal* plant which separate one plot of *kibanja* from another.

Scattered in the *kibanja* are trees planted for timber use and fuel supply. Dominant is a quick-growing tree called *omuhumula* (*Maesopsis Eminii*). The different farm units' *kibanja* plots are called *bibanja* and together form the village (*kyaro*). Throughout this book the singular form *kibanja* is used for all land cultivated with perennial crops, irrespective of whether it forms a single farm unit or a whole village (for the *kibanja* is such a distinct land-use type). From a distance the *kibanja* forming the village appears as a dense canopy of light green banana leaves, punctuated by towering dark green crowns of the *Maesopsis Eminii.*

2. Ekishambu (or Kikamba). The typology differs from the northern divisions, which primarily use the term *kikamba,* to the southern and western divisions, which primarily use the term *ekishambu.* The two terms apply to a piece of land which has been cultivated with perennial crops and has been left to be reclaimed by grass or heavy weeds. In some areas the term also applies to a piece of land which has been under seasonal crops and has also been left to be reclaimed by grass or weeds or to lie fallow. The term in this case, however, is only used for a piece of land adjacent to the *kibanja.* It may also merely mean *weed* (e.g., in Kiziba).

There are many reasons why the plot can easily change into *ekishambu.* The farm unit may be too large, so that the farmer fails to maintain part of it, or he may (due to old age) be unable to till the whole farm. Labour shortage during prolonged illness or due to death or migration of a member of the family, as in the case of a divorce, can also cause such a lack of maintenance.

Larger plots may also be abandoned to *ekishambu* because of superstition. This is often the case when,

25

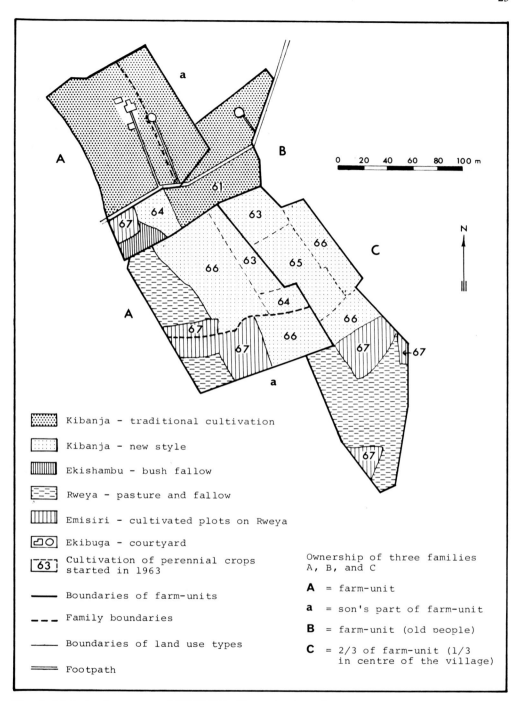

Map 3. *Main land use types. MUZINGA. Extension into the Rweya.*

26

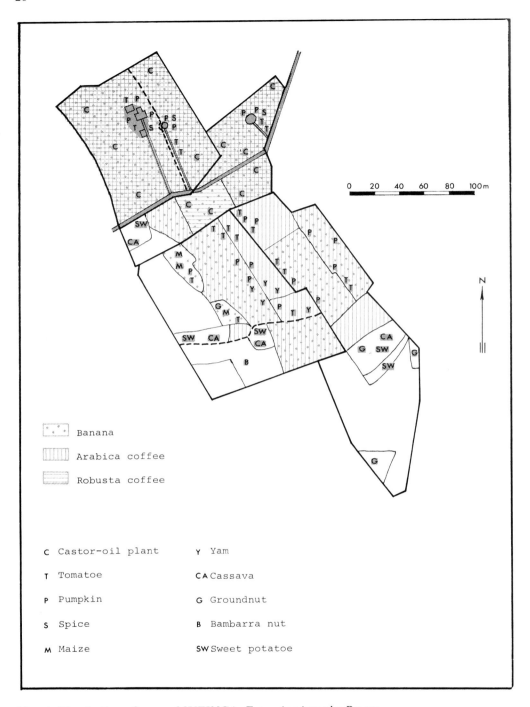

Map 4. *Distribution of crops. MUZINGA. Extension into the Rweya.*

say, a disease attacks the coffee, or for some unknown reason, the coffee trees fail to bear.

Large plots of *ekishambu* can also be accounted for by changes in ownership of the land, after which it may take some time before the new occupant manages to cultivate the entire area which he has acquired.

In the overall general land-use pattern, *ekishambu* cannot be traced either on the 1 : 50 000 maps or on the airphotos, and can be regarded as a sub-type under *kibanja*.

3. *Rweya* is the name given to open grass or bush-land. This land between villages consists of areas permanently uncultivated because of shallow soil or rock outcrops or steep slope gradients, and areas with grass fallow after the cultivation of annual crops (*emisiri*). The permanent grassland as well as the fallow land are grazed by the small herds of cattle and goats.

The *rweya* was formerly the source of fuel to the villagers, but according to Milne (1938), "the secondary bush was repeatedly cut over for fuel, and cattle and goats kept back the regeneration of the trees. The open grass-land which is a dominating feature of the present land use pattern is until now the final result of man's influence on his environment."

4. *Omusiri* is the term used for a small plot of land cultivated with annual crops outside the *kibanja*. The plural form used for several plots is *emisiri*. These plots provide the family with the necessary supplementary food. The *omusiri* plot can be adjacent to the *kibanja*, especially when the farm unit is on the outskirts of the village and still expanding into the grassland.

The *omusiri* is mainly on the *rweya* grassland and the distance from the house of the farmer to the *omusiri* plot varies from one to six kilometres, due to the shifting cultivation system and increasing population pressure.

The shifting system allows for a cultivation period of 12 to 18 months (i.e., two to three cultivation seasons) and a fallow period from 3 to 8 years (sometimes up to 12 years). The variation in the fallow period depends on differences in soil fertility and population pressure.

The crops grown are groundnuts, bambara nuts, beans, sweet potatoes, yams, cassava, sorghum, finger-millet and maize. There are different successions, but the opening crop is mainly a *leguminosae* crop.

As mentioned on page 19, the major part of the *rweya* in the littoral region is part of the grass fallow within the *omusiri* system, so grass fallow and *rweya* are hardly distinguishable on the airphotos ex-

cept by using stereophotogrammetric equipment. The *emisiri* plots appear as small squares of lighter colour if the photos are taken during the dry season, due to lesser moisture content in the plots compared with the surrounding grassland. In the field the *emisiri* plots often appear as one large field, as the women like to cultivate close together.

An example of the three main land-use types is shown on the airphoto, page 28.

Location of main land-use types
(Environmental constraints)

On pages 11–15, the variations in soil types and soil depth were mentioned, and on page 19 the relationship between rainfall and land use was pointed out. Thus the morphology of the Bukoba landscape and the resultant soils and their depths give rise to a unique pattern of land use, which Allan (1965) has described as "islands of high fertility with intensive cultivation in a sea of infertile grassland."

From the topographic maps the island pattern of the *kibanja* land-use type is obvious. On these 1 : 50 000 map sheets the location can be traced, but to facilitate the understanding of the relationships between morphology and location of *kibanja*, four profile-sections are drawn from the Lake shore towards the west. They are all drawn through the sample areas selected for the research in this book.

The profile also gives some impression of the environmental conditions for the Bahaya farmers by showing the constraints of land to the north compared with the south. The following table gives the proportional differences in land potential between the profiles from north to south:

Table 4. *Land potential in percentages of 40 km long profile sections*

Profile sections	Land mainly under cultivation	Land not used. Dry basin	Swamp	Forest reserve	Lakes
I	35	–	28	37	–
II	58	8	34	–	–
III	56	14	–	–	30
IV	75	25	–	–	–

Section I, the northern part through Kanyigo, was first settled when people came to Bukoba District and is one of the most densely inhabited areas.[5] There is no room for expanding agriculture at all unless swamp reclamation takes place, which is a very dubious enterprise at the present economic level of agriculture.

Section II, across the Bukoba town, shows the location of the regional service centre. The low-lying areas of sandy lacustrine deposits to the east are the residential quarters for Government officials, and the harbour facilities. The main problem is the periodic rise of Lake Victoria, which causes flooding of the harbour and the low-lying residential quarters.[6]

For agriculture, the limiting factor is again the swamps. It can be seen how farmers have advanced to every bit of elevated land in the swamp areas, an indication of the pressure on land, as communication to these islands is nearly impossible during the rainy season.

A third of the Ibwera section (Section III) is covered by lakes. (If the cross-section were moved 3 km to the north, it would yield only 10 per cent more land used mainly for agriculture.) Here, as well, the farmers have moved towards the west and have settled on the east-facing slopes, where the uplift of the air-masses from the trade-winds produces some precipitation.

Section IV, the Nshamba section, is so far south that swamps and lakes are not constraints. Thus it is mainly the distribution of rainfall which at present limits possibilities for agricultural expansion here. The uplifted plateau is the most densely populated area because of its broad level surface. (This section is indicated on Map 2.)

Location of villages

After considering the environment to be exploited by the farmers, we shall now examine the location of the villages, which is the same as the location of the *kibanja,* as this land-use type constitutes the villages.

The preferred location sites are the level plateau surface and the gently rounded ridge tops (marked *a* on the profiles drawings) with a sufficient soil depth. These sites were doubtless settled first, and the main roads, too, follow the north–south direction of the ridges and run along their tops.

The second location is on the slopes. Here the site chosen depends on the form of the slope, i.e., convex or concave. On the convex slope, the deepest soil is found on the upper part of the slope and at the lower level. On the concave slope, the upper part mainly consists of rock outcrops, and the soil depth increases the further one moves down the slope; so that the soil will often have a considerable depth in the valley bottom due to the eroded material which has been transported downwards. The finest material will be transported the greatest distance, so that a succession of soils with different textures will be found down the slope. Thus soil on the middle of the concave slope mainly has the texture of a loamy sand or a sandy loam, whereas the soil on the valley bottom has a texture of anything from sandy clay to heavy clay or peat.

We thus find villages located on the upper part of convex slopes (marked *b* on the profile drawing), primarily on the part with a gentle gradient; due to land shortage, however, slopes with a gradient of 20° are now under use. (See example, section III b.1.)

The concave slope is often found near escarpments. Thus the village can be located under the escarpment or under a steep hillside. The gradient and the soil depth determine the location, but it is characteristic that the villages seldom continue down into the valley bottom. (This location is indicated with the letter *c*.) If the village is located in a valley bottom on the profile it is because the traverse cuts through the extreme upper part of the valley (e.g., c.1.).

It should be emphasized that only the location of *kibanja* or villages is under discussion here. The cultivation of annual crops, the *emisiri,* can be found nearly everywhere today, regardless of slope gradient.

An important location factor in African farming systems is the siting of water supply for domestic use, especially when the water must be transported by the people themselves. Thus, consideration of factors such as fertile soil and water supply arises in establishing the village.

In Buhaya the village is identical to the area in which the perennial crops are grown, with the houses scattered all over the area (see the airphoto, page 29). The dominating location factor is, therefore, the soils.

Furthermore, the littoral region, with its well-distributed rainfall, has numerous seasonal and permanent streams and springs. The permanent streams are indicated on the profile drawings, and a land-use map for Nshamba main village (Map 5) in the plateau area shows the variation in distances to water-collecting points. The average distance during the wet season is 1 km, and this increases to 3 km during the dry season. It should, however, be noted that during the rainy season most of the water is collected from the many corrugated-iron roofs in the village, thus reducing the time spent on water collecting.

To sum up, the importance of the littoral region is underlined by the study of the profiles. The very limited possibility of expansion is obvious in the eastern part of this region. The constraints of rainfall distribution appear, and the District also faces a problem of

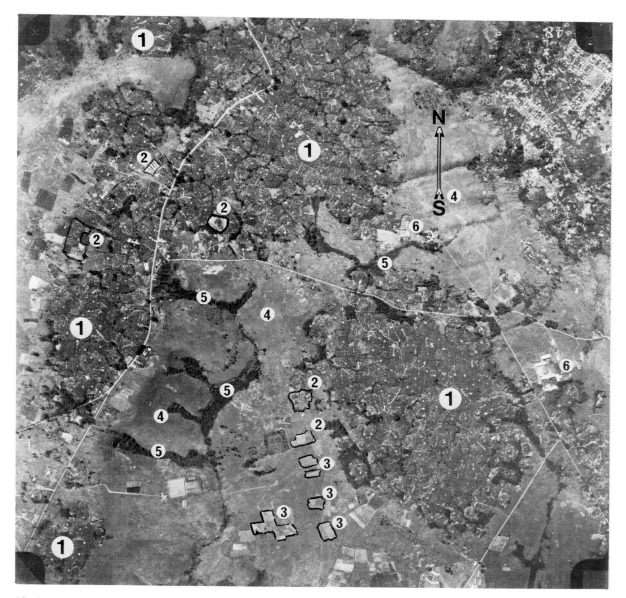

Airphoto: *Land use pattern near Bukoba town. June 1967.*

1. *Kibanja* areas cultivated in the traditional way form several villages on the photo. The small white spots in the *kibanja* areas are the corrugated roofs of the house. The *kibanja* is densely populated. The white lines are the footpaths leading to the houses.
2. *Kibanja* cultivated in the modern way, mainly monoculture of banana, because the farmers live near the market in Bukoba town. A section of the town can be seen in the northeast corner of the photo.
3. *Omusiri* fields on the *rweya*.
4. *Rweya,* the grassland between the *kibanja* villages. The major part of this area is with grassfallow after *omusiri* cultivation. The photo reveals how the *kibanja* expands into this land use type.
5. Black belts in the *rweya* are water: streams with dense vegetation.
6. The larger buildings are schools or hospitals.

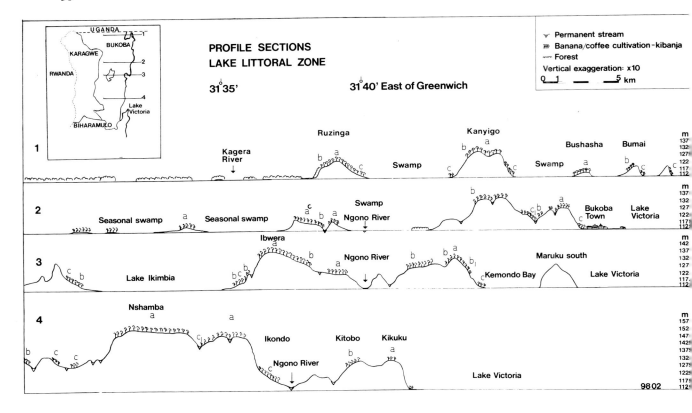

PROFILE SECTIONS
LAKE LITTORAL ZONE

31°35'   31°40' East of Greenwich

Permanent stream
Banana/coffee cultivation = kibanja
Forest
Vertical exaggeration: x10

communication from east to west during the rainy season, because the roads pass through the swampy valley bottoms.[7]

The village location is determined by topography and soil depth deriving from the erosion of the landscape and the consistency of the parent rock material.

Sample areas selected for studying the land use

The sampling

To study the land use in Bukoba three sample areas were selected by means of multistage sampling techniques. The District was divided into three areas according to the following criteria:

(A) Age of villages
    Degree of fragmentation

1. First- and second-generation farmers
2. Second- to fourth-generation farmers
3. More than fourth-generation farmers

(B) Land availability
    and population density

1. Land shortage non-existing
2. Land shortage starting
3. Land shortage acute

(C) Level of education

1–2. General
3. High level, due to mission schools started here

The three main strata were confined within division boundaries. These divisions were again stratified according to field experience so that marginal areas were avoided and strata would represent smallholder farmers with both cash crops and subsistence crops, i.e., coffee-growing was an integrated part of their farm enterprise.

Thus, three subdivisions emerged and within these the enumeration areas from the 1967 census were used as sample frames. The subdivisions were Kanyigo, Ibwera and Nshamba, and from each subdivision an enumeration area was selected at random. For all enumeration areas lists of heads of households are available from the Statistical Census Bureau in Dar es Salaam. These lists were used to identify the population in the enumeration areas. The lists were checked with help from the Ten House Cell leaders[8] and changes in the population were adjusted before drawing a random sample of 10 per cent for two of the enumeration areas and a 20 per cent sample from the

Women returning from the
river with tins of water.

third one, which was to be subsequently used for a more intensive study of the labour input.

Altogether, 100 farm units or households were selected. Of these, 10 units dropped out for various reasons during the survey, and the total remaining population was 90 farm units: 18 from Kanyigo, 20 from Ibwera and 52 from Nshamba. For every farm unit a map to scale was drawn of all the plots constituting the farm unit, and the land use was identified. These farm-unit land-use maps were checked for changes after one year. (See Map 4, page 26.)

A single interview was conducted concerning composition of labour force, land tenure, production and extension services, farm expenditure, farm income and off-farm income. This was supplemented with unstructured interviewing about general problems and peoples' attitudes towards the present agricultural policy in the District.

In addition to the random sample six 'rich' farmers were selected in each subdivision to give comparable data, in order to throw light on the problem of economic stratification in the rural society (the Haya term used for such a farmer is *mutungi*—"the man who owns cattle"). Among the smallholders, the definition

of a rich farmer was: a farmer who has much more *kibanja* than the average farmer, who has capital available to invest in buying more farm land, manure, grass, insecticides, and who can afford to employ labour; often, he is a farmer who owns considerable head of cattle.

An effort was made to select the three sample areas in such a way that other parameters were kept constant or fairly constant. The areas have approximately the same amount of rainfall, about 1 150–1 200 mm a year, fairly equally distributed. The dominant soil in all areas is ferralsol, and the altitude varies slightly, allowing either Robusta or Arabica coffee to be the chief cash crop. We deliberately looked for areas which represented the traditional cash crop, thus predominantly confining the cash earning to coffee. The locations in infrastructure are nearly the same; Nshamba is at a slightly greater distance from Bukoba town, but this does not influence the price paid to coffee-growers, as transport costs are regulated by the Bukoba Co-operative Union.

The attempt to hold some important parameters (i.e., rainfall, soil and crops) constant yields three sets of dependent variables:

Grass bundles for sale along the roadside.

1. The age of villages is chosen in order to investigate the degree of fragmentation due to the inheritance system (see under land tenure).

2. Population density and land availability are closely related to the age of the village, and it is of interest to see how farmers adjust to the constraints deriving from the interaction between the variables.

Finally, all farmers under *nyarubanja* tenure were omitted, and only freeholders were selected. (See Chapter 3, on land tenure.)

Land use of sample farms in sample areas

As noted above, the farm unit of a Haya farmer consists of two land-use types under cultivation (the *Kibanja* and the *omusiri*) and two types of uncultivated land (the *ekishambu* or *kikamba* and the *rweya*). For the three sample areas under discussion the proportionate share of these land-use types is shown in the table below. A fifth type (called *Other* in the table), which includes trees and elephant grass, can also be identified.

Differences in Table 5 must be interpreted with cau-

tion because they are samples. As the same time several ecological factors must be accounted for. A few trends can at this stage be observed, before going into details.

Kanyigo is under population pressure, with an average farm unit of only 0.94 ha, and with only 6 per cent *rweya* land available. The *rweya* land in the sample areas is grassland adjacent to the *kibanja* land and held for expansion; as such, it is an indication of land shortage or availability.

The difference in *rweya* area between Ibwera and Nshamba may be due to the location of the sample farmers in these villages. Thus, in our sample, a relatively large number of farmers in Nshamba happened to be located on the outskirts of the village and were in their second stage of farming, where after consolidation, they had started to expand into the nearby grassland (see Map No. 5), whereas the farmers selected in Ibwera were mainly from the centre of the villages, at a long distance from suitable grassland.

Nshamba is older than Ibwera and more young people there have moved away from their fathers' farm units to establish themselves, because the portion they received from their fathers was too small.

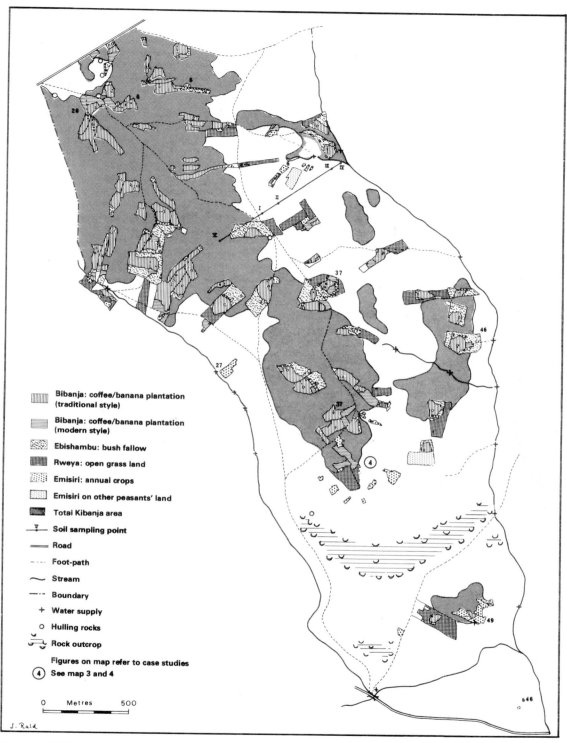

Bibanja: coffee/banana plantation
(traditional style)

Bibanja: coffee/banana plantation
(modern style)

Ebishambu: bush fallow

Rweya: open grass land

Emisiri: annual crops

Emisiri on other peasants' land

Total Kibanja area

Soil sampling point

Road

Foot-path

Stream

Boundary

Water supply

Hulling rocks

Rock outcrop

Figures on map refer to case studies
See map 3 and 4

0   Metres   500

J. Rald

Map 5. *MUZINGA & KABANGA. Land use of sample farms in Nshamba.*

34

Table 5. *Land use types—per cent of total farm unit land*

	Ibwera	Nshamba	Kanyigo
Kibanja	68.2	48.5	68.5
Ekishambu (*Kikamba*)	6.9	17.8	9.7
Omusiri	9.7	11.0	7.4
Rweya	14.4	22.4	6.0
Other	0.8	0.3	8.4
Total	100	100	100
Average farm unit	1.24 ha	1.42 ha	0.94 ha

All farm units have *kibanja*, but there is a variation in the proportion of farm units having the other land use types.

Ibwera area was settled mainly two generations ago, and the first generation claimed so much land that it can still provide for the second generation. The pressure for new *kibanja* land has not yet become accentuated.

Table 6 emphasizes, via the proportions of farmers holding *rweya* land, the difference in potential land available for the expansion of perennial crops. Nevertheless, the pattern of ownership of *ekishambu* and *emisiri* in the three areas is nearly the same. In all areas, about two-thirds of the farmers have some land lying as *ekishambu* and more than 80 per cent of all farmers cultivate *emisiri*. This shows a fairly stable pattern in the general land use.

The whole question of land-use types distribution, however, becomes more complicated when the age composition of the family labour force is taken into account.

Table 7 shows that Ibwera and Nshamba have higher proportions of male and female farmers in the most productive age group (18–40 years) than Kanyigo. A closer look at the conditions revealed that the 29 per

Table 6. *Land use types—per cent of farmers having the following land use types within the farm unit*

	Ibwera	Nshamba	Kanyigo
Ekishambu	61	61	65
Omusiri	83	86	95
Rweya	22	50	15

Trees, mainly eucalyptus trees planted for commercial use (selling as firewood), are planted by only one farmer in Ibwera and Nshamba, and by four farmers in Kanyigo.

Table 7. *Distribution of age groups in sample areas—adult men and women*

Adult men and women age group	Ibwera (%)	Nshamba (%)	Kanyigo (%)
18–40	54	61	39
41–60	17	37	46
61	29	2	15
Total	100	100	100

cent in the over 60 age group for Ibwera were mainly men with younger wives or old men living together with a son on a farm unit.

For Nshamba there was only one mother over 51 years old; otherwise, all adult women were between 18 and 51 years. Thus only half of the people in 41–60 age group were women, and the old men showed the same pattern as in Ibwera.

In both Ibwera and Nshamba there were quite a number of farm units with polygamous marriages, but in Kanyigo only one example; this difference could be due to longer influence by the Christian Church in Kanyigo.

The higher proportion of older people in Kanyigo seems to be due to the fact that young farmers migrate out of this area because of the acute land shortage. The small average farm unit (0.94 ha) and the relatively higher age of the farm population in Kanyigo would seem to correlate. All the 15 per cent over 61 years old consisted of men.

Nshamba area has 98 per cent of its population under 60, and nearly two-thirds under 40, and at the same time has the highest average size farm unit. Yet as Table 5 indicates, the larger farm unit is mainly due to the larger share of uncultivated land within the sample, namely the 22.4 per cent of *rweya* land.

The total farm unit figures can be misleading as regards production, and therefore the main land-use type for production, the *kibanja,* must be analysed further.

The distribution of *kibanja* land use on farm units

Average figures of small samples can be very misleading, and as such it is the range of farm unit sizes and *kibanja* unit sizes which is informative.

Diagram 9 gives first the distribution range for the total farm units and next for the important *kibanja* land, the land that really gives the farmers their living.

Looking at the figures on the left-hand side of the page for the farm unit size distribution, the first two columns in each figure show a characteristic evolution from a first- and second-generation village, via a third-generation village to a village many generations old.

For all three areas more than 50 per cent of the farmers' farm units are under 1.6 ha. Nevertheless, the distribution varies. In Ibwera (Fig. 1 a, Diagram 9) 60 per cent of the farmers moved into the area in the late 1920s and early 1930s, and they are now well-established farmers over 60 years old, or sons around 20–40 years old. The fragmentation of land with perennial crops due to inheritance has only taken place once, so that 89 per cent of the farm units are between 0.8 ha and 1.6 ha. This could be due to the fact that a fairly large proportion of the farm unit consists of unused land, but Fig. 1 b shows that the majority of *kibanja* farm units fall into the same ha-group.

The change in the two first columns of Fig. 2 a and 2 b (Diagram 9) from Nshamba compared with Ibwera shows a trend towards smaller farm units, especially for the *kibanja* units, where 79 per cent of the farmers have less than 0.8 ha under perennial crops, compared with the Ibwera farmers' 34 per cent. The much more normal distribution of farm units in Fig. 2 a, however, shows that more potential unused land is available. This is supported by Tables 5 and 6, where it is seen that 40 per cent of the land in Nshamba is not in use at present, as it lies either as *ekishambu* or *rweya,* and half of the farmers have *rweya* as part of their farm unit. (See Map No. 5.)

Nshamba is in a transition stage, where fragmentation and diminishing of *kibanja* land has led to the beginning of an expansion. It should nevertheless be noted that in the 1960s migration took place from Ngara to Nshamba, accounting for 10 per cent of the farmers, and these have affected the percentage of farmers with small *kibanja.*

Kanyigo, in Fig. 3 a, shows decreasing farm unit size and the village is more than five generations old. But the figure must be compared with Table 4 to illustrate the problem of land shortage. The Kanyigo farmers cannot make adjustments for diminishing farm units by expansion in their own area; their only adjustment lies in emigration by their sons. Thus some of the farmers in Ibwera came from Kanyigo area around 1935.

The *kibanja* distribution in Kanyigo, Fig. 3 b, is nearly identical with that of Nshamba and, although

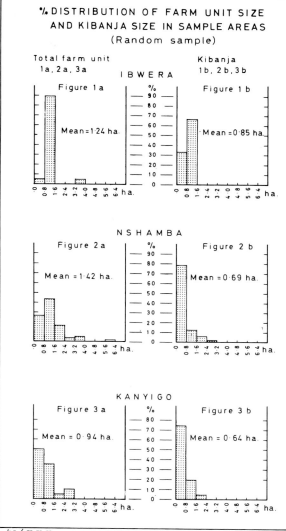

Diagram 9

the sample is very small in each case, there is a striking identity when the *kibanja* distribution in Figures 2 b and 3 b is further broken down to show the distribution of farmers cultivating less than 0.8 ha (Diagram 10). Fifty per cent of the farmers from Nshamba and Kanyigo have a *kibanja* unit of between 0.4 ha and 0.8 ha (1 acre and 2 acres), with a mean of 0.64 ha and 0.69 ha, respectively. The farmers cultivating less than 0.4 ha fall into three categories: single people, very old couples and farmers with other employment, for whom farming is merely for subsistence.

Thus one can cautiously interpret the Kanyigo fig-

36

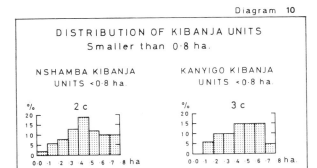

Diagram 10

DISTRIBUTION OF KIBANJA UNITS
Smaller than 0·8 ha.

NSHAMBA KIBANJA
UNITS <0·8 ha.

KANYIGO KIBANJA
UNITS <0·8 ha.

k r / m m m

greatly. Taking *kibanja* plus *ekishambu* as total *kibanja* land, the following table shows the proportion of the total *kibanja*, which the *ekishambu* constitutes, thus showing how much of the best potential land for perennial crops is available.

Table 8. *Per cent of Ekishambu in total Kibanja. Range in size of Ekishambu plots*

		(ha)	Mean (ha)
Ibwera	9	0.01–0.5	0.14
Nshamba	27	0.01–2.2	0.41
Kanyigo	12	0.01–0.4	0.14

For Ibwera and Kanyigo the possibility of growing more bananas and coffee through utilizing *ekishambu* is limited, but the Nshamba farmers holding *ekishambu* can increase their *kibanja* land by an average of 0.4 ha (one acre) on the best potential land.

Omusiri

The cultivation of the annual crops outside the *kibanja* area (see page 27) is performed by more than 80 per cent of the farmers in all three areas (Table 6) and the proportion of land used for *omusiri* does not vary much from area to area (Table 5). Taken as a proportion of total cultivated land, i.e., *kibanja*+*omusiri*, the differences between the areas become clearer.

The great range is due both to social factors (e.g., number of wives in the farm unit) and to the succession of the crops.

Table 9. *Per cent of Omusiri in total cult. area. Range in size of Omusiri plots*

		(m²)	Mean (m²)
Ibwera	13	50–2 500	1 450
Nshamba	18	150–6 500	1 800
Kanyigo	10	30–1 800	800

Rweya

It is necessary to distinguish between *rweya* held as part of the farm unit (the *rweya* in Table 5) and the grassland between the villages, which is not part of farm units. The farm unit *rweya* forms planned expan-

ures and the Nshamba figures by saying that the minimum unit of land with the perennial food crop, bananas, which can support a family of two adults and 3–5 children, is somewhere in the range between 0.4 ha and 0.8 ha, depending on the ratio of interplanted coffee (the average family in Nshamba consisted of 4.38 persons, counting only persons staying on the farm, and not including children away in boarding schools, etc.).

Furthermore, it seems possible to assume that if a majority of the *kibanja* farm units have diminished through dividing ancestors' land to a unit size less than 0.8 ha, the farmers start to make adjustments either by migrating or by expanding; at around this unit level the next division of the unit among sons will not be able to allow for pieces of land large enough to support even a young married couple. (See Diagram 11.)

Ekishambu

On page 24 *ekishambu* was defined as a sub-land use type under *kibanja*, being a piece of land formerly cultivated with perennials but temporarily not maintained and lying in weeds. Thus *ekishambu* represents potential *kibanja* land which can quite easily be put back into use. The range of the sizes of the individual *ekishambu* plots is considerable, varying from 0.01 ha to 2.0 ha; the locational distribution also varies. As Map No. 5 from Nshamba area shows, the greater part of the Ekishambu belongs to the larger farms in the southern part of the village. Most small farms are found in the northern part of the village, which is the oldest part and thus belongs to the type of farms divided up through several generations.

Around two-thirds of the farmers in the sample areas (Table 6) have *ekishambu*, but the possibility of expanding *kibanja* land by utilizing the *ekishambu* varies

sion areas (i.e., it is considered potential land for expanding the perennial crops) whereas the remaining *rweya* land can either be used for *omusiri* crops or grazing. (See also chapter 3 on land tenure.)

Land use by selected rich farmers in sample areas

The criteria for selecting rich farmers are mentioned on page 31. The final selection emerged by asking the smallholders in the samples and afterwards checking at the coffee society by asking the officials there. The suggestions were almost identical.

For the three sample areas the proportional share of the land-use types on the farm units are shown in the table below.

There is some displacement in the weight of the different land-use types: the *kibanja* area thus takes a greater share of the farm unit in Ibwera and Nshamba. For all areas it seems that the rich farmers invest less labour in cultivating the annual *omusiri* crops, which may be due to more labour-intensive cultivation techniques of the *kibanja*.

Kanyigo area has considerably more land under trees (mainly eucalyptus), than the other areas. Because of the very steep slopes in the sample areas, farmers have started to plant trees on the slopes which cannot be used for agriculture. At the same time the trees form a new cash crop because of the increasing shortage of firewood.

The distribution of *kibanja* land on farm units

1. For Ibwera it was found that all the random sampled farmers' *kibanja* land was under 1.6 ha per farm unit. As for the rich farmers, 5 out of the 6 had *kibanja* units larger than 1.6 ha, and ranging up to 5 ha.

2. Nshamba random sample farmers had 92 per cent

of their *kibanja* units under 1.6 ha whereas 5 out of 6 of the rich farmers had *kibanja* units larger than 1.6 ha, and ranging up to 5 ha.

3. 95 per cent of the Kanyigo random sample farmers had *kibanja* units under 1.6 ha, and 75 per cent under 0.8 ha. The 6 rich farmers found there range from 0.9 ha to 2.2 ha, with 4 farmers having over 1.5 ha.

Old and modern *kibanja* cultivation

A general trend is that the rich farmer is a farmer with more *kibanja* land under cultivation that the average smallholder. More important is the difference in husbandry of the banana/coffee cultivation. As mentioned on page 24, two cultivation methods are found. Thus the *kibanja* land-use type can be divided up into: (1) old cultivation of banana/coffee (*ukulima wa kawaida*) and (2) modern cultivation of the same crops, the so-called *ukulima wa kisasa*.

In the old *kibanja* cultivation bananas and coffee are grown in mixed stands. There is no fixed spacing between the banana stems and the coffee trees, and consequently there can be anywhere from 1 000 to 2 000 banana clumps per hectare and 250 to 1 000 coffee trees per hectare, depending on the proportion between the bananas and the coffee in the mixed stand.

The modern cultivation methods apply mainly monoculture of the two perennial crops, with a fixed spacing allowing for 750 banana clumps per hectare and 1 350 coffee trees per hectare. Some farmers prefer to use a compromise, whereby they keep the regular spacing but plant 3 lines of coffee trees, then one line of bananas, and so on.

Whereas the old *kibanja* is mulched with banana stems and leaves, the modern *kibanja* is heavily mulched with grass, which is cut on the grassland or bought. The coffee trees are pruned and sprayed regularly. Thus the modern style is more labour-intensive,

Table 10. *Rich farmers. Percentage of total farm unit land.*[a] *Land use types*

	Ibwera	Nshamba	Kanyigo
Kibanja	79.9 (68.2)	60.2 (48.5)	65.4 (68.5)
Ekishambu	4.7 (6.9)	2.2 (17.8)	10.8 (9.7)
Omusiri	4.7 (9.7)	7.1 (11.0)	1.4 (7.4)
Rweya	10.7 (14.4)	26.9 (22.4)	10.0 (6.0)
Other (mainly trees)	– (0.8)	3.6 (0.3)	12.4 (8.4)

[a] The figures from the random sample of farmers are given in brackets.

Table 11. *Types of Kibanja cultivation: Percentage of total Kibanja areas*

Kibanja Cultivation methods	Random-sampled farmers			Rich farmers		
	Ibwera	Nshamba	Kanyigo	Ibwera	Nshamba	Kanyigo
Old	86.6	82.3	83.5	44.6	57.0	47.0
Modern	13.4	17.7	16.5	55.4	43.0	53.0
Total *Kibanja*	100			100		

which also means that is is more capital-intensive, as capital is invested in hired labour.

Because a greater share of the *kibanja* land of the rich farmers is under modern cultivation methods, as compared with the random-sampled farmers, it has implications for the understanding of changes in the Bukoba farming.

Less than one-fifth of all the random-sampled farmers' *kibanja* area is under modern cultivation method, while half of the rich farmers' *kibanja* is cultivated in the modern way. We shall later break down the figures for modern cultivation into three different groups, but to understand how the different characteristics between rich and 'common' farmers have emerged, we must look at the land tenure, land allocation and agricultural extension policy.

Summary

The main features of the environment for Haya farming have been outlined. By describing the distribution of soils, morphological forms of the landscape and the rainfall distribution, the main ecological zone in Bukoba District, termed the Lake Littoral Zone, has been demarcated.

The conditions of the environment have served as background for the understanding of the land-use pattern: an island pattern with the villages located on the deepest soil, where they maintain an intensive cultivation of perennial crops surrounded by extensively used grassland. Nevertheless, all the land-use types are integrated into the Haya farming system, consisting of cultivation of perennials, annuals (in a shifting cultivation system) and animal husbandry. Every type of land use is dependent on the others in such a way that the fertility of the *kibanja* area is maintained at the expense of the intervillage grassland.

The functional aspect of the land use of farm units in selected sample areas, representing different stages of village development in age and different environmental conditions, has been analysed. From a human ecological point of view the importance of the *kibanja* land-use type has been stressed, and the constraints and possibilities for adjustments to the pressure on land have been dealt with.

Thus far the focus has been merely on the physical factors of the land-use aspects, although some social factors have been touched upon. Using the term 'the functional use of land', our objective is to apply the land use analysis in a much broader sense, taking social, economic and political factors into consideration.

The next step in the analysis of Haya farming must be to review the land tenure system and the agricultural policy applied on Mainland Tanzania, and especially how this policy has been implemented in pre- and post-independence Tanzania in Bukoba District. The functional land-use pattern reflects not only the physical features of the environment, but also the motivations and implications of the rules and actions of different institutions, such as traditional land tenure, the Ministry of Agriculture and Bukoba Co-operative Union.

Tanzania today champions a socialist policy with special emphasis on the rural sector. This policy may lead to major changes in Haya farming with or without conflicts. To illuminate this important stage of Haya farming, it is necessary to give a thorough analysis of the traditional land tenure system and how it has developed recently. Finally, the agricultural policy for extension service applied over the last 70 years will also be considered.

Notes

1. With the traditional system of dividing the father's land among the sons, the fragmentation rate is very fast and in some areas to the north there is less than one acre (0.4 ha) per household, which can just maintain a minimum subsistence level of production, but allows no land for cash crop development.

2. The four terms applied here to the whole district differ slightly from subdivision to subdivision, but apart from the term *ekishambu*, all clans have agreed that the three main terms are applicable throughout the District. The variation in terminology will be dealt with under land tenure.

3. To the north and north-east in the District, in Kiziba and Bugabo Divisions, a *kibanja* should also contain a few bark-cloth figtrees. (Bark-cloth fig=*Ficus Natalensis Hochst.* In Kihaya=*Orubugo* or *Mrumba*).

4. Throughout this book the crop in general is referred to as bananas. When certain subspecies are discussed they are referred to with a functional adjective, i.e., cooking, beer, roasting and sweet bananas.

5. On the middle slopes of the Kanyigo ridge, both to the east and the west, old caves with Stone Age paintings are found.

6. Suggestions to move the harbour facilities 16 km south to the Kemondo Bay have been submitted to the Ministry of Lands (S. Jensen, 1968).

7. In 1968 many feeder roads were impassable and during the long rains of March–May the main road to Uganda (the Kyaka road) was twice closed for 20 miles, so that people had to be ferried in dugout canoes.

8. The smallest political party unit in Tanzania is the cell. A cell consists of ten houses grouped together to advance the political aims of the party at the grassroots-level and to enable them to express their views to the party and the Government. All TANU members living in those ten houses comprise a cell. Each cell elects a Leader, who takes overall charge of the affairs of the cell at the Branch Annual Conference.

Chapter 3. Agricultural Land Use and Land Tenure

In a peasant society customary law, which deals with the rights and privileges of the people within their social and political institutions, is dominated by man's relation to his environmental resources. Thus rules concerning inheritance, bride price, divorce, loans or mortgage reflect the importance of property or production deriving from the utilization of land resources. As land or different types of land, with their vegetation, are the basis for the peasant's entire life, the customary laws dealing with land tenure and thereby with the methods of acquiring land are essential for an understanding of the farming system. The interaction between land tenure and land use shows how farmers adjust to changes in their resources, such as increasing land shortage, and increases or decreases in human or livestock population. Similarly, they adjust their customary law to changes in the social framework of society; e.g., changes caused by altered values due to education.

Thus the acquisition of land under customary land tenure plays an overall important role in resource allocation and the transferral of land between individuals. Furthermore, the Tanzanian smallholder has not been much affected by either the colonial or the Tanzanian Government land legislations, which have been primarily concerned with large-scale farmers or estates.

The only legal actions causing a major change in the West Lake Region land tenure system are the three Acts of Parliament concerning the *nyarubanja* system.[1]

Nyarubanja[2]

In Bukoba there existed a feudal system of land tenure, where the pattern of holding land had assumed a hierarchical character, with the king (*Mukama*) at the apex. The hierarchy consisted of institutions of client-ship, based on land (*kibanja* land) as the most important property among the Haya (Reining).

The *Mukama* exercised rights with respect to land, allocating areas of populated *kibanja* to individuals of the ruling class. People living on these areas became tenants (*batwarwa*) of the individual landholders (*batwazi*). There are two main views on the origin of this institution. "The institution arose from the *voluntary* act of many original settlers of Buhaya giving themselves and their properties up to the Bahinda [the ruling dynasty]. The Bahinda were a group of pastoralists who had come to Buhaya from Bunyoro to settle." The other, contrasting theory, which appears more plausible and is supported by Cory, is that of conquest of the indigenous rulers by the Bahinda. "The invading conquerors", he says, "became the absolute masters of the conquered people and their lands." (James, 1971.)

As the concern of this book is mainly the present land-use system, we must refer readers to the four authors mentioned in note 2 for a study of the development of *nyarubanja*. In effect, only approximately 10 per cent of the holdings in Buhaya were under *nyarubanja* (Mutahaba, 1969). The rest were what Reining calls 'owner-occupants' or what Mutahaba terms 'freeholders'.

Integration of cattle and agriculture

The major interest of our study lies in the oral traditions about the exchange of manure and milk and the authority of land allocation between the invading Bahinda and the indigenous people.

The oral traditions hold that at the time of the arrival of the Bahinda, the indigenous people were agriculturalists growing crops like millet and yams —that is, agriculture based on annual crops and even perhaps shifting cultivation methods.

The availability of cattle manure as a supply for the sandy soils of Bukoba apparently facilitated the cultivation of bananas as the staple food. Bananas were certainly grown and appreciated by the indigenous people, but on the unfertilized sandy soils the bananas had such a low yield that they could not form the staple food.[3] By applying manure to the bananas the yield was increased to the point where the households could obtain sufficient food from a small area of banana cultivation.

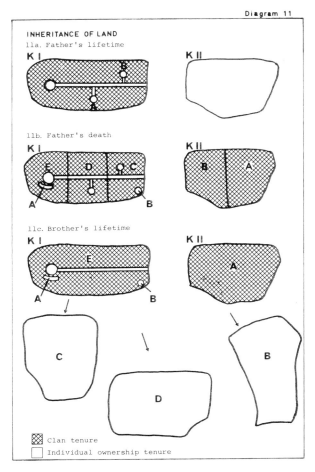

Diagram 11

INHERITANCE OF LAND

11a. Father's lifetime

K I   K II

11b. Father's death

K I   K II

11c. Brother's lifetime

K I   K II

▨ Clan tenure
☐ Individual ownership tenure

At the same time the semi-permanent settlements of the millet growers gradually shifted to a permanent settlement pattern. The land tenure also gradually changed from usufructuary ownership to proprietary ownership. Thus, "the effect of Bahinda's settlement was definitely not the suppression of the agricultural culture of the indigenous population. It was to result in the blending of the two cultures, the agriculturalists becoming also cattle herders, and the herders in turn taking on agricultural traits." (Mutahaba, 1969.)

With the introduction of coffee as a cash crop interplanted in the banana *kibanja,* the *kibanja* land-use type ·grew more important and strengthened the proprietary ownership right. Coffee cultivation also encouraged the minority of landholders to extend their control of *kibanja* land through the *nyarubanja* system.

The *kibanja* became the important land-use type, and the following case study will show how allocation of *kibanja* land through the mechanism of inheritance within customary laws aims at keeping *kibanja* under the control of the clans.

An example of customary land tenure and the mechanism of inheritance

In our examination of the basic elements of customary land tenure in Bukoba, a single family case will be described first.

Five brothers, A, B, C, D, and E, at a mature age of between 30 and 50, were all living on well-established *kibanja* farm units in 1970. How did they acquire their land?

Their father had a fairly large *kibanja* when they grew up during the 1930s. This is marked K.I and with a hatched signature in Diagram 11 a. In this *kibanja* was the *nyaruju* (the family house), where the nuclear family lived together. The family consisted of one mother and daughters, in addition to the above-mentioned male members. The daughters played no role in the question of acquiring land in this case.

The K.I *kibanja* (hatched signature) was inherited by the father from his father and was under the rules of family tenure. This is called 'clan land' (*kibanja ky'oruganda*). This plot can only be acquired by inheritance, and transfer to others than heirs can only be done with the consent of the nearest members of the clan. (*Orukiiko lwo oruganda* = clan council.)

When the boys grew up, the father moved to another area 10 km away, where he acquired a piece of *rweya* from the chief and paid an allocation fee of 5 shs to the Native Authority. The father then converted this *rweya* land to *kibanja* by planting perennial crops. This K.II *kibanja* was regarded as being under individual ownership tenure, i.e., it can be sold or transferred to other individuals without interference of family or clan members. (Yet everyone knew, of course, that the father was only expanding for the good of his sons, and he would have been considered completely insane if he had transferred the K.II to anyone else.)

Son A and son B married before the father died and stayed in the father's first *kibanja.* They had their own houses, however, with the paths from these houses joining the major path leading from the father's house and out of the *kibanja.*[4]

When the father died, the two pieces of *kibanja* were divided as shown in Diagram 11 b. Son A and son B shared K.II in nearly equal portions; A, as the primary

Kibanja under clan tenure. The tomb of the owner's father is seen in the foreground to the right. In the background to the left an old Haya hut.

heir (*musika*), got slightly more than B. C, D and E divided K.I in three equal portions; the youngest son, the second heir (*mainuka*), received the portion with the family house, but all of the three youngest sons stayed together with their mother as long as they remained unmarried. At the time of the division of the first family *kibanja* after the father's death, the two oldest sons received a symbolic piece in K.I as well, with A again receiving a piece slightly larger than than of B. In fact, B only got one coffee tree's space.

When C and D were about to marry, they 'sold' their portions to the youngest brother, E, and each of them bought a piece of *kibanja* in the same village on which to settle down. They had to sell their parts officially to the youngest brother to avoid later claims from their future children, but they were paid less than the market value of the land. During this time B sold his part of K.II to A and also bought his own piece of *kibanja*. Thus, in 1970 all five brothers, by mutual help and transactions, are well established on their own *kibanja* land, but A's and E's *kibanjas* are under clan or family tenure, whereas those of B, C, and D are held under individual ownership. (See Diagram 11 c.)

When the five plots of *kibanja* are divided among the heirs at the death of the brothers, the land of A and E will remain under clan tenure, and the land of B, C, and D will be converted back to clan tenure. Thus the

mechanism of inheritance is to expand clan land and stress the importance of *kibanja* land, which is the bearer of both the main food crop and the main cash crop.

The main pattern of allocation of land within the customary law has been shown in this example. In general, it is not particularly important that some of the land acquired by the brothers was *rweya* land, because in due time it was converted into *kibanja*. That is only a matter of economics. If a farmer can afford it, he prefers to buy a developed piece of land instead of starting from scratch on grassland.

This example gives the main theme in the transfer of land and land tenure; it is, however, a theme with numerous variations from one former chiefdom to another. The role of the heirs changes from one area to another, as well as according to whether the predominent marriage system is monogamous or polygamous. In Kanyigo (Kiziba), the succession of heirs differs from Ibwera (Kianja) and Nshamba (Ihangiro).

In the preceding example the first son was the primary heir and the youngest son the second heir. The idea behind this seems to be that the youngest brother will probably be unmarried when the father dies, while the brothers who have already married are provided for. The youngest son is then taken care of by the mother and *vice versa*. The youngest son will call the mother

Traditional Kibanja. Along the footpath to the right the boundary plant: Dracaena deremensis. =Ekihanyi. See also the text, page 24.

his "wife". This assumption of responsibility for the mother will depend on the age of the youngest son.

In the case of polygamous marriage the inheritance interests of both wives must be considered. In such a case the oldest son of the first wife is the *musika* (primary heir) and the oldest son of the second wife the *mainuka* (secondary heir).

It has been said above that the right to use and transfer land takes different forms in different divisions (particularly in former chiefdoms). Before independence, the chiefs were the main authorities responsible for the allocation of land. With the abolition of chiefdoms after independence, however, the responsibility of allocating land was taken over by the administration, at the local level under the control of the Village Development Committee (VDC.) VDCs were set up all over Tanzania in 1962 and 1963 as development institutions at village level, promoting communication from below to above and *vice versa*. The Village Branch Chairman of TANU was appointed chairman of the VDC and the Village Executive Officer (normally the former parish chief) was appointed Secretary.

The other members of the VDC consisted of the chairmen of the Ten House cells. The VDC existed up to 1969, when it was supplanted by the Ward Development Committee.

Göran Hydén (1969) notes that "To a large extent, parochial attitudes have always prevailed among the leaders of the VDCs and the party cells." Concerning land allocation the political influence in the VDC did not make any impact, as it merely became the administrative organ for allocating unoccupied land formerly held by the chiefs and now claimed as Government land. Furthermore, in the 1960s the TANU officials at village level in Buhaya were merely informative links between District and Regional TANU institutions, rather than innovators actively initiating changes in rural society.

The three Acts of 1965, 1968 and 1969 which suppressed the interests of the landlords and broke up the feudal system have had the greatest effect on land tenure in West Lake.[5] It should be remembered, however, that the *nyarubanja* system was not found in Karagwe, a neighbouring District of Bukoba. In the rest of West Lake, as well, only one-tenth of the farmers were considered to be under *nyarubanja* tenantship. Nevertheless, the importance of the abolition of the landlords lies in the fact that they often held the best coffee land.

Thus, at the beginning of the 1970s the majority of Bukoba banana/coffee smallholders lived under a land tenure system partly consisting of customary laws and partly of Government regulations, partly administered by individuals, partly by clan members and partly by Government administrators.

Disputes about land are taken to court and appeals can be made through all courts to the High Court. The whole problem of land tenure has become more complicated since the introduction of the cash economy at the turn of the century. Pledge and mortgage, often followed by land transactions, have become common. At the same time, with the development of the cash economy, the selling of land has grown to high proportions.

Cory and Hartnoll (1945) write:

Sale of land was practically unknown until within the last forty years and therefore no rules were evolved by customary law to deal with it. Even now the cases (court cases) are comparatively few, so that no law adequate to social and economic life has come into being. Such rules as do exist have arisen to meet outstanding demands at one time or another, and are in many instances illogical and contradictory and may easily fail to cover a particular situation.

It is doubtful whether the last part of the statement is valid; it depends on the standard of measurement. It is more likely that the rules emerging had to fit in with customary laws as well as with regulations exercised by British-educated magistrates; it is thus hardly surprising if contradictions arose.

Land tenure characteristics

Table 12 is an attempt to show the relationship between land tenure, land use, and the mechanism of acquisition. The arrows in the table show how land, sooner or later, returns to clan control.

Table 12 shows that African land tenure is dynamic. It deals with the situation that pertained in 1970. In the previous decade, the following changes had taken place:

(i) Landlordship—tenantship had been abolished (due to the nation's socialist policy and the legislation deriving from this policy).

(ii) Administration of uncultivated land, *rweya,* had been transferred from the chiefs to the Government (due to the abolition of the chiefdoms). There is no longer any allocation fee. Officially all land belongs to the Government; the farmers have the usufructuary rights of occupancy.

If we look at the last 70 years, we shall find that the cash economy made a major impact on the land tenure system, as this economy is dependent on a perennial crop—coffee (and later tea).

Pitblado (1970) has observed that: "In general, there is a progression from usufructuary ownership to proprietary ownership as cash crops are introduced, perennial crops planted, and other pressures on the available land increase." This applies to Bukoba, where cattle became an integrated part of the farming system on the arrival of the Bahinda. The cattle manure made possible the shifting from annual crops to the perennial bananas as the dominating food crop and the establishment of permanent fields, the *kibanja* fields. At that time, customary land laws made adjustments to secure the tenure of *kibanja;* the elaborate inheritance rules have further emphasized the importance of *kibanja.*

When coffee was introduced as a cash crop, it was naturally interplanted with the bananas already growing on fertile soil, and proprietary rights within the clan system were protected by demarcating *kibanja* boundaries with plants or trees. The introduction of a cash economy made a major impact on land tenure, as the chiefs manipulated the *nyarubanja* system to obtain tighter control over *kibanja* land and thereby the important cash crop coffee.

Flexibility in customary laws

We have only outlined the major trends in the land-tenure and land-use relationship. Nevertheless, customary laws have numerous adjustments to meet individual cases and the transfer rights within individual teure are flexible, e.g., a nephew may be allowed to inherit his uncle's *kibanja* if the uncle has no children. (Often there can exist a closer relationship between uncle and nephew than between father and son.) Even a friend can be allocated a piece of *kibanja,* if this friend has helped the deceased during his lifetime. Daughters have—at least for the last fifty years—been able to acquire land from their fathers, particularly in emergency cases, such as if they are still unmarried upon the death of their father, or in a case of a divorce where the daugher has no male children from the divorced husband.

The need to keep the *kibanja* in the family-clan tenure arises in the few cases where the primary heir is not 'trustworthy or mentally balanced'. The father can then decide that the second son shall inherit the father's main *kibanja.* The second son may, however, refuse to take over this *kibanja* to avoid straining relations with his elder brother. In other cases he will accept the heritage or even demand it. The father eventually decides to adhere to custom, but gives the untrustworthy first son only a symbolic share, such as the banana trees around the tomb or around the house, while the main part of the *kibanja* will go to the faithful son, so that the land can remain under clan tenure.

The power of the clan is also seen from the fact that the 'clan-council' (*orukiiko lw'oruganda*) can overrule the decisions of the deceased person if they endanger the interests of the clan land or if the record of that particular son is tainted with ill-fame.

Class formation and acquisition of land

The ecological system of Bukoba District, with its variation in soil fertility, increase in population and consequent shortage of fertile land, contains factors which have led to great emphasis being placed on the importance of securing rights to *kibanja* land. At the same

Table 12. *Land use related to land tenure. Bukoba smallholders*

Land use	Clan tenure	Individual tenure	Government
Kibanja (mainly perennial crops – banana and coffee)	*Acquisition* (a) By inheritance (b) Allocation by consent of clan members.	*Acquisition* (a) By purchase (b) Allocation by Government (deserted *kibanja* with no claim from clan).	*Acquisition* Deserted *kibanja* with no clan claim: Government takes over. Formerly taken over by the chief.
	Rights of use (c) Proprietary rights within the unwritten rules of the clan (d) Usufructuary rights for family members according to head of family decision.	*Rights of use* (c) Proprietary rights within individual ownership rights: freehold.	
	Transfer rights Within lifetime of holder, sale requires consent of clan; at holder's death transfer to heirs according to customary clan laws. Dividing among heirs.	*Transfer rights* Within the owner's lifetime free disposal At owner's death land goes back to clan tenure and follows customary laws, inheritance and dividing among heirs. ⟵	*Transfer rights* Allocation to individuals. Application required. ⟵
	Heirs Male and female. (Formerly only males could inherit immovable property).	*Heirs* As under clan tenure: male and female.	–
Ekishambu	Like *kibanja*	Like *kibanja*	Like *kibanja*
Rweya	*Acquisition* Like *kibanja a* and *b*. (This kind of *rweya* is mainly adjacent to the *kibanja* and considered potential *kibanja* land).	*Acquisition* (a) Purchase (b) Allocation by Government on Government *rweya*.	*Acquisition* Unused land formerly held by the chiefs now held by Government.
	Rights of use (c) Free grazing rights for all cattle owners (d) *Omusiri* cultivation: permission of holder; usually contribution to holder from crop (e) Cutting grass: permission of holder.	*Rights of use* (c) Free grazing rights for all cattle owners (d) *Omusiri* cultivation: permission of owner contribution to owner (e) Cutting grass: permission of owner.	*Rights of use* (c) Free grazing rights for all (d) Free *omusiri* cultivation to all (e) Free cutting of grass for all.
	Transfer rights Same as under *kibanja*	*Transfer rights* Within the owner's lifetime free disposal At owner's death land goes back to clan tenure ⟵	*Transfer rights* ⌐ Allocation to individuals. Allocation to *Ujamaa* villages ← Application required.
	Heirs Male and female	*Heirs* As under clan tenure.	
Omusiri	No special tenure for *omusiri* plots, as they are temporary and part of the *rweya* land use pattern. For rights of use, see under *rweya*.		

Modern farming near Bukoba town. Monoculture of banana background and foreground to the right. In between a field with tea cultivation.

time the socio-economic pattern has evolved towards increasing individualism in relation to land.

In post-independence Bukoba the hierarchical control of land executed formerly by the kings and the *nyarubanja* landlords has broken down, but a new rural elite which has strong links with the former hierarchy has emerged. The core of this elite contains businessmen and educated people.

A new house with corrugated roof. In the background the old Haya hut, now used as kitchen. In front of the house a drum for collecting rainwater.

The rapid rise in coffee production, the booming of its price on the world market in two periods and an ensuing drastic fall, and the organization of coffee marketing have given rise to the formation of two particular groups in this elite. The first is a small group of businessmen, who manipulate the coffee economy through trading, smuggling, bribery and corruption, combined with money-lending at exorbitant interest rates. (For further analysis of this part of the Bukoba economy see Chapter 9.) These people are the real exploiters of the farming system in Bukoba and they are normally not greatly concerned with the acquisition of land. The second and by far the largest section of the economic rural elite consists of a group of rich farmers who are also either small-scale businessmen or wage-earners. The order of the combination should indicate that the rich farmers use an income derived from non-farming activities to expand their farm-unit areas. The wage-earners include people employed outside agriculture, civil servants, clergymen, cooperative officials, managers, shopkeepers, etc. These people invest the surplus from their salaries or allowances in farming in their home areas.

The common feature of this large group is that in one way or another these people have capital available from work outside their own farm unit, and this capital is invested in expansion of the farm areas and/or improved agricultural husbandry. The objectives, apart from an improved standard of living, are basically the same as those mentioned above: to provide for their children in the future, as some of them will have to rely on agricultural production to earn their living. Again, to invest in agriculture, say, by buying *kibanja* land, is also a method of meeting the obligations to family members. Every wage-earner in this country feels the heavy burden of these obligations: the requests for school fees, covering of hospital expenses, repayments of loans, help with clothes and everyday necessities such as salt, sugar, tea, meat, etc.

The sphere of responsibility and the number of dependent relatives or clan members can increase considerably when a person with a monthly salary is transferred to his home area. The degree of burden these social obligations confer can be seen from the following example.

A civil servant in a fairly good position became very ill. During his illness his relative came to see him to ask for a little economic support. When the relative was asked to come back after the civil servant had recovered a bit, he was furious, and went back to their home village. There he went around in the village tel-

ling everybody what a bad person the 'rich' man was. "He could not even give me 20 cents for buying salt, I will never receive him in my house and I do not even want him to attend my funeral!"

A lot of what could be termed 'exploitative' requests can be dealt with according to the wage earner's own judgement, but situations constantly crop up where the society, without having to make any formal request, expects a contribution from the 'rich' person, if that person wishes to maintain good relations with his relatives and friends.

One way of dealing with these family obligations is to invest money in *kibanja* land in the home area. This land can be allocated to poor relatives, an aunt or divorced sister, who maintain it and at the same time obtain their subsistence.

Furthermore, in a young nation like Tanzania, the land thus bought gives security, like an old age pension. The civil servant can retire to his *shamba* at home and in his old age enjoy the close social contact with his own society after the alienated town life.

Thus, the elite not only accumulates wealth, but a substantial part of this wealth is reallocated for the benefit of the family in the context of traditional *ujamaa* customs.

The elite's impact on land acquisition

This process of class formation in rural areas has a major impact, not only on income distribution, but also on the distribution of the best land.

The importance of the money economy with regard to land tenure and the possibilities of land transfer are shown in Table 13.

Table 13. *Methods of acquisition: per cent kibanja plots in sample areas*

	Inherited from father	Obtained by purchase	Allocated by Native Authority[a]	Allocated by VDC[b]
Ibwera	50	39.5	7	3.5
Nshamba	48	24	21	7
Kanyigo	75	22.5	–	2.5

[a] Native Authority was the chief's representative dealing with allocation of mainly uncultivated land before independence. Normally a fee of 5 shs was paid (Ekishembe).
[b] Village Development Committee.

From the table it can be seen that where land shortage is really an acute problem, there are only two methods of acquisition, inheritance and purchase. As the division of *kibanja* land through inheritance diminishes the size of the units of this land available for the heirs of the coming generations, the only adjustment to this situation within the customary framework is either expansion through purchase of land or migration.

Table 13 also shows that the Government Agency for allocating land since Independence (the VDC) has played a very limited role in the sample areas, indicating that in the densely populated Lake Littoral Zone of Bukoba District there is not much potential Government land available for expansion of perennial crops.

Nevertheless, it was shown in Table No. 5 (land-use) that the *rweya* land within the total farm-unit area ranged from 6 per cent to 22 per cent. This *rweya* land, which is also part of the *omusiri* fallow system, is held under clan tenure or individual tenure and, as Table 12 shows, this land is held to provide for the owner's children in the future and will in due course be converted to *kibanja*. Although all land not planted with crops belongs to Government, the VDC has been very reluctant to allocate this *rweya* land to smallholders.

To convert *rweya* land to productive *kibanja* demands a heavy capital input of manure and grass mulch. Furthermore, if the conversion scale is to be on the order of ½ hectar per year, only the elite can afford it, as it needs the use of hired labour. It should briefly be noted here that one of the basic factors in the development of this rural elite is the availability of a large migrant labour force from neighbouring countries (especially Burundi) at a wage rate of shs 1/50 to 2/– per day. (See page 94.) Establishing new banana or coffee plantations on *rweya* land on a large scale costs from 2 000 to 4 000 shs. per acre (0.4 ha), which limits this enterprise to the people with capital, as long as the farming system is on an individual basis. This means that the "rich" farmers can expand more rapidly than the very small holder using only his family labour.

Impact of land shortage on rural inequality

When good *kibanja* land becomes scarce, the price of land goes up. Table 14 shows how the market value of *kibanja* land has increased during the last 20 years.

In the Ihangiro sample 31 farmers out of 52 had bought one or more plots of the main land-use types to expand their farm units. Very few farmers in the sam-

Table 14. *Increase in market value of well-established Kibanja land 1950–1970 (Ihangiro)*[a]

Year	Shs per ha	Shs per acre
1954	3 000/–	1 200/–
1960	4 000/–	1 600/–
1965	5 420/–	2 168/–
1968	7 400/–	2 960/–
1970	10 000/–	4 000/–

[a] The prices are average calculations.

ple had sold land. This raises the questions: which farmers are selling land? What is the mechanism in the demand for and supply of land?

There are two main reasons for a farmer to sell all or part of his land:

1. To move to another area because of population pressure on land. In that case the small holder will often start by selling one-third of his *kibanja* to get some capital on which to survive during the first period of hardship in opening up new land. Over the following period of establishment he will rely on part of his former *kibanja* for food supply and gradually sell the rest. In that way, in densely populated areas in Bukoba District a considerable amount of developed *kibanja* will be available for the well-off farmers to purchase. At the same time the very small holder mainly producing for subsistence will be pushed out towards marginal areas.

2. To clear debts. A lot of short-term loan transactions occur in Buhaya rural society. If the debtor cannot repay his debts at the agreed date (e.g., when the final payment of coffee drops considerably), the loan is normally prolonged for a short period, but at very high interest rates, e.g., equivalent to 200 to 400 per cent per annum. The final solution to clear the increasing debt may be to sell the land and migrate.

Thus, selling of land is often connected with migration of the poorer farmers as an adjustment to economic crisis. The purchase of land as an adjustment to land shortage works in favour of the rich farmers, who gain more control over the fertile and already developed *kibanja* land. In this way the formation of a rural class structure has been supported and the gap between the rural elite and the majority of common farmers has been growing, creating an inequality in the distribution of not only income but also of fertile land.

Nevertheless, certain factors in the social structure of the society and in the natural resources have kept the class formation in Bukoba below a certain level.

Even though the Haya farming system has developed according to an individualistic and capitalistic pattern, there are striking features of clan control in the socio-economic structure of the Haya village which are antagonistic to this pattern as far as land is concerned.

1. *No speculation in land.* There is no speculation in land in the normal Western capitalistic sense of the word, i.e., holding unused land for the speculative purpose of gaining an economic profit from the increasing price of land, or buying *kibanja* land for later speculative sale. The speculation in buying land is concerned with the means of providing sufficient *kibanja* or potential *kibanja* land for one's children, so that they will be able to get a decent start in life.

The attitude codes of the rural society within the clan structure to land use and land tenure prevent the individual from purely economic speculation in land. The inheritance system limits the expansion of land through purchase to the lifetime of an individual, because division of the property will take place when the individual dies.

2. *Resource constraints and technological level.* It has been pointed out in the first chapters of this book that the potential resources are limited, which means that a supply of fertile *kibanja* land on a large scale does not exist. Nobody can, e.g., invest 20 000 shs in *kibanja* land in one year; instead he has to expand over the years in bits and pieces.

Furthermore, labour and level of technology, which are the other resources available, set limits to the size of farm unit a farmer can maintain.

We have often heard the statement from rich farmers when discussing land expansion: now I have got enough to provide for my family, and this is what I can afford to maintain properly.

3. *Social and political insecurity.* Within the last few years (since 1968), the Government's drive towards a socialist transformation of rural society has created an atmosphere of social and political insecurity among farmers in Buhaya as a whole. Concerning land, this insecurity has led to an attitude of wait-and-see. In particular, the takeover of houses in May 1971[6] has led almost to a standstill in expansion of land through purchase and also in other investments such as cattle and improved housing.

This insecurity, which often is due to lack of understandable communication of the *ujamaa* message from civil servants and Tanu officials, has given rise to the circulation of all kinds of rumours, like: "Government wants to pool all the farm units together", "the coffee prices are going down because Government uses the surplus for *ujamaa* villages", "Government will soon take over our cattle", etc. This rather hostile or sceptical atmosphere can, however, switch from one day to the next. A certain ward got a water supply in May 1971. The same month the final payment for coffee was announced and it turned out to be higher than for many years. People in that ward now praise the wise leadership of President Nyerere and want the M.P. for that area to be their representative forever, because these good things have come during his time in office.

A major issue for all farmers—even very small holders—is the question of land for their children. The basic question dealing with the foundation of life for Bahaya farmers—the rights of the clan to transfer and acquire land within the framework of customary laws—has been shaken, and even the very small holder feels that his freedom to choose his own way of living will be hampered. He does not realize that under the present socio-economic system his individual freedom to choose is a delusion.

Furthermore, there is no real awareness of being exploited among the very small holders, partly due to the many mutual links between rich and poor, partly due to the large labour force of migrants coming from outside and partly due to the fact that the smallholders still has the choice of two alternatives. These alternatives are: 1) to be "exploited" by working for the rich farmer and thereby obtain an immediate profit or 2) the laborious and long-term way of developing and expanding his own farm unit with the help of his own family labour.

In the context of the socialistic policy of Tanzania, all land officially belongs to the Government and the Haya farmer has only the rights of occupancy arising out of customary laws. Nevertheless, the majority of the farmers in Bukoba District utilize land held under either rights of clan ownership or rights of individual ownership. This fact must be considered seriously when trying to transform the Haya rural society into communal farming activities.

Notes

1. *Nyarubanja* Tenure (Enfranchisement) Act 1965, Customary Leaseholds (Enfranchisement) Act 1968, Customary Leaseholds (Enfranchisement) (Amendment) Act 1969.

2. For a detailed analysis of *nyarubanja*, the reader is referred to four authors:

Cory and Hartnoll (1945)
Priscilla Copeland Reining (1967)
Gelase R. Mutahaba (1969)
R. W. James (1971)
(see bibliography).

3. This has been observed in *ujamaa* villages which have planted bananas without manure.

4. The term *nyaruju* indicates that the first family house is the house of importance. Nya=mother, original or big. The courtyard in front is called *ekibuga* and the footpath from the *ekibuga* is termed *eilembo*. When the sons obtain their own houses with their own *eilembo*, the father's footpath changes to the term: *nyarulembo*=the mother of . . . Formerly, the term *nyarulembo* was mainly used in connection with the *ekibuga* of the *omukama* (the king). In some parts of the District the *eilembo* can be a rather broad road leading to the *ekibuga*.

5. In 1971 a Commission was still dealing with the compensation claims from the landlords.

6. The Acquisition of Building Act, 1971.

Chapter 4. Animal Husbandry and Land Use

The introduction of cattle

Cory and Hartnoll write:

The great landmark in the history of Uhaya is the arrival of the Bahinda about three hundred and fifty years ago.[1] ...

... The introduction of cattle on a large scale produced an economic revolution in land tenure. Because the Bahinda practice of farming out cattle made it possible to cultivate bananas on a much larger scale because of manure.

The Bahinda brought two innovations: 1) The introduction of chieftainship superimposed on the clan structure, which they allowed to continue and made use of in their political system of indirect rule; 2) The introduction of cattle-breeding.

In former times the chief alone disposed of cattle. From his spoils of war, from his own herds etc. he distributed beasts among his relatives, favourites and prominent soldiers. . . . Although for the last 50 years everyone has been allowed to own cattle, the original descendants of these recipients are still the richest cattle owners. (Cory & Hartnoll, 1945, p. 167.)

Animal husbandry and land use

It has been mentioned that cattle are an integrated part of the Bukoba farming system (page 39) and that the Bukoba soils as such are poor. It seems likely that a system of exchange between the invading pastoralists and the agriculturalists in Bukoba District evolved, so that the pastoralists received bananas or other agricultural products in exchange for manure and milk (Mukurasi 1970).

Although an outbreak of rinderpest at the end of the 19th century killed about 90 per cent of the cattle population, estimated at that time to be about 400 000 head (Friedrich 1968), mixed farming has continued to play an important role in maintaining the fertility of the soil and increasing the production of bananas and coffee.

In 1970, 72 000 head of cattle were registered as being dipped regularly. After the dipping charge of ten cents per head was removed in mid-1969, the farmers have responded with great enthusiasm to the dipping scheme. In 1970 there were 51 Dipping Centres in Bukoba District. The 1967 census counted about 100 000 peasant households in Bukoba District; from the three sample areas in 1968–1969, the percentage of households keeping cattle was: Ibwera 22 per cent, Nshamba 21 per cent and Kanyigo 15 per cent. Taking 20 per cent as a District average, this amounts to about four head of cattle per household, which fits in with Friedrich's figures from 1968 (see table p. 51). A detailed investigation into the composition of the average herd for Nshamba in 1968 yielded the following figures:

Of the 18 rich farmers selected in the sample areas, 11 kept cattle, ranging from 4 to 30 head per household; six of them had more than 10 cows.

It has not been possible to verify the statement by Cory and Hartnoll that the recipients of cattle from the former kings are still the richest cattle-owners. In the 1970s, many cattle-owners have relatively large herds of cattle, due to income from sources other than their own agricultural work.

Other factors, however, show the importance of cattle as related to land tenure and land use. Of the 20 per cent of the farmers in the samples, all belonged to the group of farmers with more than 0.8 ha of *kibanja*.

Farmers use two *debe*[3] of manure[4] for every coffee tree, or 2–4 *debe* for every banana plant when they plant. One sack of manure costs 3 shs (1970 price) and contains 6 *debe*, so if a farmer wants to plant 0.4 ha (one acre) with coffee in the modern style, he will use 180 sacks of manure to the value of 540 shs, and will need up to 1 080 shs worth for one acre of bananas.

Table 15. *Livestock population 1958–1970 (Bukoba District)*[a]

Year	Cattle	Sheep	Goats
1958	50 339	39 116	35 940
1960	60 217	17 264	40 188
1965	66 400	19 000	44 000
1970	78 000	11 000	31 907

[a] *Source:* Veterinary Office, West Lake Region, March 1971.

Calf sucking after the milking is finished. In the background cattle-shed with corrugated roof. The young man to the left is employed by the owner sitting in front.

Cattle laws

The main purpose of keeping cattle is to obtain manure; this is also seen from the many laws concerning transfer of cattle between individuals.

As only every fifth household keeps cattle, the distribution of cattle manure should be limited to those who can afford to buy either cattle or manure. To adjust the situation resulting from the scarcity of cattle, the Bahaya have a system of transferring cattle to friends and relatives. As cattle are very closely related to the owner, the system is rather a mutual service than a leasing of the cattle (Friedrich 1968)[5] even when the owner receives a reward in kind, such as beer or agricultural products from the subsistence sector of the farming.

Table 16. *Composition of average herd of sample household*

Nshamba	Number of head per household	Per cent
Calves under three years	1.4 (0.7)[2]	26
Heifers and cows	2.7 (2.8)	50
Bulls and oxen	1.3 (0.5)	24
	5.4 (4.0)	100

During the time the cattle are kept by the friend, he has the right to use the manure and the milk. If the cow produces a calf, the latter may be "returned" to the owner, but the owner must in any case be informed immediately.

A cow or a head of cattle can also be owned communally by two or more farmers. In such cases, the owners keep the cow in turns, each period being arranged according to the size of the share the members have in the cow. During his turn each member has exclusive use of manure and milk.[6]

Animal husbandry

To obtain as much manure as possible, the cattle are kept in the shed or the *boma* for about 14 hours per day. Cows are usually taken out for grazing at around 9 a.m. and returned before 7 p.m. in the evening, when it gets dark. The journey to the grazing area often takes up to an hour, so that the cattle graze around 8 hours daily; with the present pasture, this is not sufficient to keep them in good condition, and they are normally given no additional fodder in the shed. At present, 1.2 ha of pasture is available per head of cattle.

The pasture consists mainly of various species of *Digitarium, Eragrostis* and *Hyparrhenia, Loudetia* and *Brachiaria*. Some species could provide valuable feed if regularly grazed, but under the present system where cattle owners act as herdsmen strolling in turn all over the *rweya* to find good grasses, the good species quickly become rank and tough and are then avoided by the cattle (see picture).

The *rweya* is burnt over annually in an attempt to get rid of these unpalatable grasses during the dry season. This practice is, according to some experts, of dubious value, however, as long as the burning is not controlled, since the new shoots are eaten very quickly and the soil is exposed to soil erosion from trampling by the cattle, so that the pasture is hardly improved.

Population pressure and animal husbandry

Every village has a cattle headman. He is the responsible leader for the cattle-owners who graze their cattle communally. The cattle headman makes the daily decision as to where the herd is to graze, and he has certain claims on the *rweya* grassland.

He can, in co-operation with the VDC and the village headman, restrict the *omusiri* cultivation on the *rweya* if he considers this cultivation to interfere too much with the available pasture area. The *rweya* is not divided into certain grazing areas. All villagers can graze their cattle throughout Buhaya, whether the grassland is publicly or privately owned. People from other tribes also have free grazing rights in Buhaya.

Longhorned Bukoba cattle on the Rweya.

With increasing population pressure the farmers take more and more *rweya* land under *kibanja* cultivation, and the demand for making available *rweya* land for *omusiri* cultivation also goes up. With expanding cultivation of the perennial crops, banana and coffee

Cattledip in Ihangiro. Once a week the peasants can have their cattle dipped. From August 1969 this service is free of charge.

The herd returns in late afternoon hours to the village. The cattle are of the Ankole and East African Zebu type.

(*kibanja*), the demand for cattle manure (which is so essential for the leached and eroded *rweya* soil) is rapidly increasing. A growth in the cattle population is necessary if the demand is to be met, but such a growth faces the problem of a continuous reduction in the grazing area available. Furthermore, this reduction will affect the best *rweya* soil first.

In view of the poor quality of the pasture, the trend towards importation of improved cattle stock aggravates the already low carrying capacity of the grassland.

It may be foreseen that new methods of animal husbandry will have to be introduced, such as improved pasture, change in the grazing system and stall feeding. This again requires adjustment of the rights on the *rweya* land.

Summary

Cattle form an integrated part of the farming system, and animal husbandry is not under the strict control of the clan system. Cattle were introduced and allocated by chiefs to farmers on a basis of relationships between friends or administrators, and which cut across clan lineages. Grazing rights were not restricted, and herding was done communally. Thus, animal husbandry is related to public land tenure under Government administration, and is customarily done on a communal basis; hence it is one of the agricultural activities where

the *ujamaa* policy can more easily make progress, as for example in co-operative dairy units and *ujamaa* ranching schemes.

Notes

1. The Bahinda originated from a Hima dynasty in Bunyoro and Ankole in Uganda. This dynasty can trace its history back to the invasions of a pastoral people from the north-east of Africa. The Hima clan, the Bachwezi, was followed by another Hima clan, the Baiito. One clan member was Igaba, whose son Ruhinda migrated south and became the chief of Karagwe and Ihangiro. Later, the other chiefdoms developed from the Ruhinda clan, with the exception of Kiziba. The Baziba claim to descend from another son of Igaba, named Kibi. (Cory & Hartnoll, 1945)

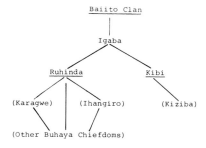

2. The figures in brackets are from Friedrich's table (1968) of the livestock composition on farms keeping cattle, from a sample of 120 farmers in the District.
3. A *debe* is an empty 4-gallon kerosene tin=approx. 27 lb.
4. *Manure* is throughout this book used to designate cattle dung (in

54

quotations also called FYM=Farm Yard Manure). Green manure is called *compost* and artificial manure is called *fertilizer*.

5. Friedrich p. 183: "The old principle of rewarding faithful servants has been replaced by a system of neighbourly leasing of cattle. The hire of cattle has to provide the hirer with stable manure for his banana land."

6. The most common breed is the longhorned Ankole and East African Zebu type. They are low milk-yielders, usually producing 1 to 2 pints daily (1 pint=0.57 l.). Since 1970, however, improved stock has been imported from outside the region by the BCU, both to sell to farmers and to establish *ujamaa* dairy units.

Chapter 5. The Policy of Agricultural Extension in Bukoba

The agricultural extension policy in West Lake dealing with coffee/banana cultivation has mainly been concentrated in Karagwe and Bukoba Districts. Although we here are only dealing with the present Bukoba District, we must remember that before 1957 the two northern districts were together called Bukoba, and much of the policy in pre-independence days applied to both Karagwe and Bukoba Districts.

During the *German Period (1884–1916)*, the German administrators and the White Fathers missionaries encouraged the growing of *Robusta* coffee on a commercial basis, and introduced the growing of *Arabica* coffee. The Germans also attempted to force the chiefs (kings) to give up their privileges of growing coffee and parcel out the cultivation to their subjects. Thus coffee cultivation on an individual smallholder basis started, but it was *involuntary*.[1]

The *British Period (1916–1961)* started with an even stronger enforcement of expanding coffee cultivation. In 1916 the administration made it compulsory for each family to plant 100 coffee trees among their bananas. Although the resentment against this innovation was widespread (old farmers still remember how chiefs and peasants were beaten when they resisted), the production of coffee in Buhaya (Karagwe and Bukoba) increased rapidly from 493 tons in 1910 to 10 882 tons in 1935 (see Diagram 12).

Until 1936/37, the agricultural policy of the colonial administration was that of quantitative measure, and no qualitative measure was imposed on the farmers. This extension of the coffee production was followed by rather favourable coffee prices up to 1934, and the decline in quality was balanced by greater output. With declining prices and ever-worsening husbandry, however, the British administration launched a policy of improving coffee cultivation by modern agricultural methods. Native Coffee Boards were established in 1936 and in the "Coffee (control and marketing) Ordinance" of 1937, the legislation was laid down which was intended to allow the administration to accomplish the objectives of crop improvement.

Three major issues of improvement were controversial for the farmers: 1. uprooting old unproductive coffee trees and replacing them with new seedlings; 2. immediate uprooting of the banana stem when the banana bunch was harvested (to eradicate the banana weevil which was at that time causing serious damage to banana production);[2] 3. heavy mulching of that part of the *kibanja* where the coffee trees were growing, using both banana stems and grass.

Although these three methods of improvement were sound from an agricultural point of view, and have been applied by many farmers since independence, not only did they create resistance due to the customary relations between the two perennial crops, but also the attempt to enforce the methods on the farmers, combined with punishments (fines) for those who disobeyed, aroused a political activity in which land tenure and the relations between chiefs and farmers and the administration and farmers were completely disturbed. To illustrate this we quote two authors:

> . . . the British began at this time campaigns to increase the coffee production in the Bukoba area. For this reason, regulations concerning inspection and scientific methods of improvement had to be implemented. According to the principle of indirect rule, the chiefs were first approached. If the British could get the authority of the chiefs behind the scheme, certainly people would accept it. On this issue, however, the chiefs themselves were reluctant. They feared far-reaching changes in land tenure—the British had passed the law abolishing the right to create new 'nyarubanja' holdings in 1936. . . . With no real support from the chiefs and without any consultation of the local people, the project was doomed to fail. [Göran Hydén (1969), p. 111.]

And p. 115: The Tanganyika African Association branch in Bukoba (a political organisation formed by the educated elite and the wealthy illiterate traders to promote civilization by improving public health, education and the rights of women in society. The TAA branch was formed from the former Buhaya Union and African Association which was an interreligious association based mainly on the Haya tribe) which had been activated because of the second world war, had a strong revival in the late 1940's, when Mr. Ali Migeyo took over the leadership of the organization. Again one of the main reasons for its new strength was the Haya reaction against the British plans for agricultural improvement. . . . Traditionally it was considered madness to uproot the stems of the banana. The Bahaya could not understand why this had to be done now. (p. 115.)

The farmers also suspected the colonial rulers of having introduced the banana weevil in Bukoba so that the subsequent shortage of food

Diagram **12**

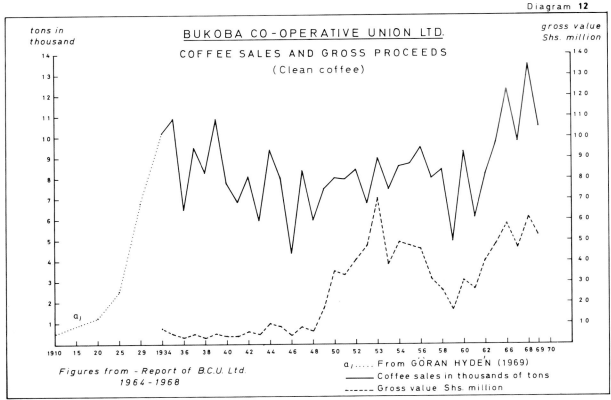

tons in
thousand

BUKOBA CO-OPERATIVE UNION LTD.

COFFEE SALES AND GROSS PROCEEDS

(Clean coffee)

gross value
Shs. million

Figures from - Report of B.C.U. Ltd.
1964 - 1968

a,...... From GÖRAN HYDÉN (1969)
———— Coffee sales in thousands of tons
------ Gross value Shs. million

kr/mmm

would make the Bahaya work for a wage to buy 'Ugali' (maize flour to cook porridge). Now the idea of uprooting banana stumps was seen as a colonialist plot to hasten the destruction of the banana crop. [Mukurasi (1970), p. 11.]

The innovations were introduced by force without any attempt to explain the benefit to the Bahaya and without any understanding of the Haya agricultural system or the social structure of the Haya society. The above detailed quotations on this issue show a classic example of how an important innovation can fail completely.[3]

From enforcement
to persuasion and demonstration

The tension between the peasants and the *Bwana Shambas* (Agricultural Field Extension Officers) grew to such an extent that in the 1950s the *Bwana Shambas* had to abandon the work in the countryside. Consequently nearly all improvements stopped and the quality of the coffee continued to decline.

Not until 1957 did the Agricultural Department change its policy and embark on an attempt to under-

stand the factors behind the peasants' resistance, and so switch over to a policy of persuasion and demonstration. The true landmark in extension service, however, came with the formation of the Bukoba Native Co-operative Union (BNCU) in 1950; a Cultural Section within this union was to be in charge of an extension service.[4]

In October 1950, 48 primary societies were registered and in 1967 this number had increased to 74 affiliated primary societies. In 1959 the BNCU controlled not only the marketing of the coffee but also the coffee-curing company BUKOP. These examples are merely intended to show the monopoly and strength of the Union, which we shall deal with later under problems of marketing. Our concern here is the Union's methods of extension and the extent to which the extension service made an impact on land use.

Immediately before and after independence the BNCU launched various campaigns to improve the husbandry of coffee (and thereby the quality of the beans), and to raise production.

In 1960 BNCU allocated 75 000 shs to "Coffee Pest Control". The Union provided trained spraying teams free of charge, while the farmers had to buy the insecticides. This capital investment and the general supersition of the farmers led to the result that mainly the 'rich' farmers benefited from the campaign. They had the money to buy the insecticides, and as we have pointed out earlier, the rich farmers are those with a relatively large *kibanja* area— that is, they could take the risk of having part of their *kibanja* sprayed, whereas the smallholder was too afraid that the new medicine would dry up his few coffee trees, and so felt that the risk was too great.

From an agricultural point of view it was unfortunate that the spraying was scattered and not systematic, as it thus had little impact on the selected *kibanja* plots, since they were small islands in the sea of unsprayed coffee. The most important thing, however, was that the farmers saw that the trees survived and even improved, so that the distrust in the extension service diminished.

After independence (1961), a campaign for coffee-tree pruning started, with an allocation of 50 000 shs from the BCU Surplus Fund. The principle was the same as with spraying. The Union provided the trained personnel and the farmers paid 10 cents in service charge per tree. Mukurasi (1970) writes,

The pruning saw was as feared as the pesticides had been in the early stages . . . They (the farmers) feared that the coffee trees would not be able to put up new branches after the pruning and that they would ultimately dry up. . . . Response was again slow . . . Finance was again a handicap . . . when the total number of trees treated is contrasted with the number of trees in the area, we find that at most 20 per cent of the trees benefited from the campaign.

Parallel with these two campaigns, the Government (through the Department of Agriculture) worked to convince the farmers to uproot old coffee trees and gradually replace them with new seedlings from BNCU nurseries. In the period 1961–1963 twenty-three nurseries were closed down due to lack of funds, and the Union remained with eleven nurseries.[5]

The distribution of coffee seedlings had started in 1957 and in 1962 a more proper husbandry for digging holes and mixing the planting soil with manure was demonstrated and recommended, but with very little response from the farmers, who could not understand the reasons for this labour-intensive work.

Table 17 shows the trend over the first three years of the spraying and pruning campaigns:

With an estimated population of more than 10 million coffee trees in West Lake, the figures show that about 10 per cent received treatment within the first three years. This seems to be a fairly good response, in view

Table 17. *Spraying and pruning campaigns—trend over the first three years*

Year	Number of coffee trees treated against various pests[6]	Sale of insecticides (shs)	Number of coffee trees pruned
1961/62	229 819	7 464	43 304
1962/63	318 189	14 776	107 521
1963/64	406 257	21 406	110 668
Grand total	954 264	43 646	261 668

Compiled from BNCU *Report 1961–1964*.

of the implications of the extension policy in the past; it should also be remembered that the farmers had to contribute to the financing of the improved husbandry. This, as mentioned before, led to the result that mainly the richer farmers benefited from the innovation. BCNU also introduced certain conditions in their distribution of seedlings from the Union's nurseries to the farmers. In co-operation with the field extension officers from the Department of Agriculture, an inspection scheme was carried out. If the farmers wanted to obtain seedlings from the BNCU coffee nurseries, they had to prepare the planting holes according to the new prescription for modern cultivation (*ukulima wa kisasa*). After inspection by the Field Extension Officer (*Bwana Shamba*), the farmer received a receipt for so-and-so many holes prepared and could then fetch the corresponding number of coffee seedlings from the nursery free of charge.[7]

The three innovations mentioned, pruning, spraying and proper planting of seedlings, all faced the same bottlenecks of the Haya agricultural system's structure: the huge area to cover (Bukoba and Karagwe Districts cover a total of 5 800 square miles = 15 016 km²); the dispersed villages, due to the ecology of the region; the structure of these dispersed villages, with the individual homesteads scattered throughout the village area; the lack of manure and cash for the majority of farmers; and the costs and difficulties of recruiting and training sufficient extension workers.[8]

Thus, the innovations did not have a widespread effect, but the importance of the first five years of improvement campaigns should not be underestimated: some of the farmers' superstition was removed and the resistance and hatred towards the staff members of the colonial Department of Agriculture was not transferred to the BNCU's campaigning staff, as the members of the societies had much more confi-

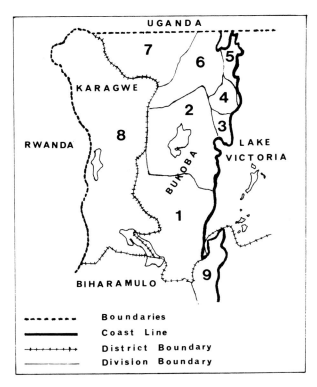

UGANDA

7

6 5

KARAGWE

4

2

3

8

RWANDA

LAKE
VICTORIA

1

BIHARAMULO

9

- - - - - - -   Boundaries
―――――――   Coast Line
+-+-+-+-+-+   District Boundary
―――――――   Division Boundary

Map 6. *West Lake Divisions of Bukoba and Karagwe.*

dence in this organization, since they obtained a better price for their coffee, due to the introduction of the final payment; the BNCU staff furthermore provided a real service to the farmers: pruning and spraying. Nevertheless, the BNCU Extension Service up to 1965 was too expensive and ran with a deficit which had to be covered from grants and other income. The spreading effect was also too scattered and haphazard, so in 1965 BNCU changed its policy of extension.

BCU Ltd. Demonstration Plots

To promote a more widespread knowledge of modern farming methods, the BCU in 1965 started to establish demonstration plots. The objectives of this change in the extension service are given in the *Report* of the Bukoba Co-operative Union Ltd. for the years 1964/65–1967/68:

The aim was to teach the farmers in a practical way the best agricultural methods of growing coffee as well as bananas.

The first plots were opened in 1965 and are wholly financed by Bukoba Co-operative Union Ltd. The idea of having Demonstration Plots situated close to the main roads, replaced that of individual shamba treatment, which had been done heretofore by BCU Cultural Section Supervisory Teams at a cost of ten cents per coffee plant.

In 1968 the Union had put up 74 Demonstration Plots in the areas where the primary societies were located. The following list shows the position and number of Demonstration Plots in West Lake Region in 1968. (From BCU *Report,* op.cit. The geographical location of the Divisions is shown on Map 6.)

The main idea was to have half an acre (0.2 ha) with traditional interplanting of coffee and bananas but maintained properly; a quarter-acre with monoculture of coffee and a quarter-acre with monoculture of banana planted with the modern spacing,[9] the planting holes being prepared with manure or compost. The two quarter-acre plots should also be heavily mulched with grass, various insecticides demonstrated, and the proper pruning of both coffee and bananas also undertaken.

The BCU approached farmers to allocate one acre of their *kibanja* for demonstration purposes. The Union covered all costs and investments needed for establishing, and the staff from the Union did the work, with some co-operation from the owner of the plot. The maintenance of the plot was undertaken by BCU for the first four-year period and then the plot was handed over to the farmer. The compensation to the farmers for uprooting and clearing their *kibanja* land for Demonstration Plots was the harvest of coffee and bananas produced on the plot. The farmer had only to keep records of the yield and the price obtained by selling the products if they were marketed.

The BCU Report continues:

An amount of shs 75 000/– deductable from final payment is annually being allocated to the Coffee Improvement Fund, solely for the purpose of Demonstration Plots.

Table 18. *BCU demonstration plots 1968*

Division	Number of plots	District
1. Ihangiro	19	Bukoba
2. Kianja	17	Bukoba
3. Bukara	2	Bukoba
4. Kiamtwara	5	Bukoba
5. Bugabo	6	Bukoba
6. Kiziba	14	Bukoba
7. Missenyi	3	Bukoba
8. Karagwe	7	Karagwe
9. Kimwani	1	Biharamulo
Total	74	

At the same time Kilimo (Ministry of Agriculture and Co-operatives) put up 11 Demonstration Plots using funds allocated from the Tanganyika Coffee Board.

The yields from these plots have been most encouraging and examples learned acted as a stimulus to some of the growers to start their own modern shambas and ask for experts' advices, where necessary.

Nevertheless, going through the recording sheets of the farmers, it was found that the recording was poorly done. Either the farmers were not able to keep statistics, or more likely they were reluctant to co-operate in that part of the demonstration work. As usual they feared to give out information about income and felt anxious about the use of such information.

There seems to have been a strange competition between the two extension agencies, instead of co-operation. The Kilimo Plots were often allocated not far away from the BCU Plots and certain recommendations from Kilimo that the Union should be restricted in its extension ambitions is reported by Mukurasi (1970). The main point in the competition from the development point of view seemed to be finance; Kilimo was allocated funds which allowed this department to set up 11 Demonstation Plots, and in 1969 they had to give them up because the funds were exhausted. The BCU could embark on a demonstration enterprise exactly on the scale they considered necessary to get a coverage of the Region, and according to their organization they were able to allocate enough money to establish very productive Demonstration Plots.

The question of competition seemed to vanish again in 1967 and a good collaboration between Kilimo extension staff and BCU took place, mainly in distributing the seedlings to the farmers after the extension staff had inspected the planting holes. Kilimo *Bwana Shambas* made the inspections, and BCU had their own *Bwana Shambas* in the nurseries to deliver the seedlings to the farmers. When the demand for seedlings increased, the BCU *Bwana Shambas* also participated in the inspection of hole preparation.

The lesson to be learnt from the years of extension work from 1965 to 1969 is: if a region has a strong Co-operative Union like the BCU, and the co-operation between this Union and the Ministry of Agriculture is smooth, much can be achieved in improving the husbandry of peasant agriculture, mainly because the Union controls the organizational apparatus to raise funds for implementing innovations, and through the primary societies they have the contact with the farmers which can be used as a channel for extension, education and the granting of credit.

To sum up: during the period 1965–1969, the following extension activities were carried out in the Region, with a dominating emphasis on Bukoba District:

BCU established and maintained 74 Demonstration Plots.
Tanganyika Coffee Board established 11 Demonstration Plots through the Ministry of Agriculture.
Maruku Experimental Station planted coffee-spraying and fertilizer trial plots in Bukoba, Karagwe and Ngara Districts.
BCU maintained 14 nurseries to supply seedlings to the farmers.
Pruning, spraying and mulching techniques were taught to the farmers by both BCU and Kilimo staff.
Hole preparation was inspected to a total of 521 915 holes in the region in 1968.
Pests and diseases like tailed caterpillar attack, coffee stem borers, leaf miner, coffee berry borers, and coffee leaf rust were treated.
Uprooting of old unproductive coffee trees took place, although these were often replaced by bananas instead of new coffee seedlings (due to price fluctuation).
Coffee husks as fertilizer were brought into use.
Seedlings supplied from the BCU nurseries increased and in 1968, 414 362 seedlings were distributed throughout the Region.

Reports from Kilimo and BCU in this period are optimistic about the farmers' response to extension, but there is a general anxiety about the declining quality of the coffee.

BCU *Report 1964–1968*, p. 19:

With the exception of the 1964/65, maganda coffee (dried cherries) delivered to the BUKOP Ltd (Coffee Curing Factory) have generally been of lower quality than expected. Consequently a new grade of Maganda known as *Rejected Cherry* has been introduced.

Cherry coffees delivered by Societies to BUKOP Ltd. contain many hollow and very small cherries which cannot easily be sorted out, and as a result the losses to BCU Ltd. are estimated at shs 200 000/– in an average season.

In the West Lake *Annual Report* from the Ministry of Agriculture, 1967, page 6, it is stated:

Extra pale bean defectives are still taking the lead and the percentage of small size beans is on the increase. The reason for the pale beans is that some growers do not carry out a selective picking of only ripe cherries and the reason for the small-size beans may be attributed to the fact that quite a number of trees are too old and also probably to varietal characteristics. . . .

It is suspected that smuggled coffee of poor quality from neighbouring countries Uganda, Ruanda and Urundi has contributed to a certain extent in lowering the quality of our coffee.

And *Annual Report*, page 15:

There is also the problem of improvement of quality. As long as the coffee here is marketed as dried cherries (maganda) it is difficult to

Table 19. *Distribution of traditional and modern cultivation of the kibanja: percentage of total kibanja area 1970. Random-sample farmers*

Types of cultivation	Ibwera		Nshamba		Kanyigo	
Traditional coffee/banana interplanted	86.6		82.3		83.5	
Modern cultivation: coffee monoculture	–		7.5		8.6	
Modern cultivation: banana monoculture	3.3	13.4	1.6	17.7	3.8	16.5
Modern cultivation: coffee/banana	10.1		8.6		4.1	
Total cultivation	100		100		100	

assess its quality and our extension effort to advise on improvement of quality will be hindered by the fact that there is no price differential between coffee (in this case dried cherries) which has been properly picked and dried and that which has not. Only when a solution is found for a price difference, will the farmer feel that all was worth the effort.

[The falling coffee prices throughout the 1960s have also had an impact on the farmers' efforts.—Authors' comment.]

The farmers I interviewed also expressed the concern over the fact that they were being paid the same price for their well-cared for, capital intensive coffee, like the traditionalist farmers. It is lack of price differentiation the farmers contended that was in a way limiting the expansion of modern farming for the unprogressive farmers see no incentive (financially) to make them change their farming way.

[The authors have often during their interviewing heard the same refrain, that the carrot held in front of the farmer to persuade him to change to modern farming must be not only the promise of a higher yield but also a better price for a better quality.]

The biased benefit of the Extension Service

It has been argued in the previous chapters that the so-called traditional agricultural system, upon the introduction of the monetary economy, has widened the gap between the few rich farmers and the many poor. Several authors argue that the agricultural extension policy of BCU has been mainly in favour of the rich farmers (Hydén and Mukurasi and indirectly the *Annual Report for 1968* from Kilimo). All agree that the

response from farmers to the methods of improved farming in the modern way has been increasingly positive, but lack of finance has held back the very small peasants from participating.[10]

To investigate whether this trend is valid or not we shall analyse the random-sample farmers in Bukoba District and compare them with the sample of the 'rich' farmers. First, have the Demonstration Plots and the work of extension staff had any impact on the land-use pattern of the *kibanja* cultivation, combined with the fact that good seedlings could be obtained only if the new technique of modern cultivation was adopted?

By comparing the two tables, one perceives an obvious difference in the degree to which the average farmer and the 'rich' farmer have adopted the modern cultivation technique. Now, the area unit figures could be quite misleading, if for example only one or two farmers within the random sample had accounted for all the cultivation in modern style. Nevertheless, the following table shows that the response to improved methods over the last five years has been quite satisfactory for the very small farmers, and a glance back to Diagram 9 on page 35 shows that more than 90 per cent of the farmers concerned have less than 1.6 ha of *kibanja*.

The majority of the farmers have adopted modern cultivation when they have expanded their *kibanja* area onto either former *ekishambu* land or *rweya* land; only a few of the 'rich' farmers have uprooted old coffee trees and changed the old *kibanja* to modern *kibanja*.

Table 20. *Distribution of traditional and modern cultivation of the kibanja: percentage of the total kibanja area 1970. Rich farmers*

Types of cultivation	Ibwera		Nshamba		Kanyigo	
Traditional coffee/banana interplanted	44.6		57.0		47.0	
Modern cultivation: coffee monoculture	11.7		20.9		18.0	
Modern cultivation: banana monoculture	2.3	55.4	6.3	43.0	25.4	53.0
Modern cultivation: coffee/banana	41.4		15.8		9.6	
Total cultivation	100		100		100	

Table 21. *Percentage of farmers who have done some cultivation in modern style since 1955*

	Random Sample	'Rich'
Ibwera	44	100
Nshamba	50	100
Kanyigo	30	100

This applies mainly to the 'rich' Kanyigo farmers,[11] who have embarked recently on expanding monoculture of bananas because of the fairly good market price and their own means of transport, as they either have their own cars or have access to cheap transport.

As the figures in Tables 19 and 20 express a ratio of expansion, it can be seen that 30–50 per cent of the very small farmers have expanded their *kibanja* area with 13–18 per cent, which in absolute figures means a range from a few hundred square metres up to 1 ha, whereas all the 'rich' farmers have expanded about 50 per cent, ranging from ¼ ha up to 2 ha. To this should be added that some of the 'rich' farmers have expanded by buying traditional *kibanja* land from other people.

Extension of bananas in the modern style cultivation. The new suckers are planted in lines with proper spacing.

Coffee Arabica. Cultivation in modern style. Coffee trees planted in lines and well pruned. The ground is heavily mulched with grass. In the background pineapples under the trees.

Costs and activities involved in modern farming

The BCU Demonstration Plots proved to the farmers that with sufficient input of capital in the form of labour, manure, fertilizer, grass-mulch and insecticides, the Bukoba soil could give substantial yields of coffee and banana. In particular, it was proved that by capital-intensive proper husbandry, the time from planting to the first yields of coffee and bananas could be speeded up, so that coffee would begin to bear after 3 to 4 years (formerly up to 8 years) and bananas would yield their first bunches after 12 months (formerly 24 months).

Yet very little was published and known to the farmers about the cost of this modern farming. From the BCU accounts we find that the establishing and maintenance costs at the end of the 1967/68 financial year for the 74 Demonstration Plots were shs 298 806/–, that is, on the average, shs 4 000/– capital input over the first two years for one acre of coffee/bananas in the modern style.

It is thus no wonder that *ukulima wa kisasa* (modern farming) on a relatively large scale was closely connected with the so-called rich farmers, the people with income sources from work outside agriculture: school teachers, pastors, house constructors, BCU officials, magistrates, civil servants and other wage-earners, plus the coffee traders and moneylenders.

The very interesting point, however, is that even the very small farmer struggled to cultivate on modern lines, even if his cultivation amounted to one-tenth of an acre per year. On the other hand, a farmer wishing to expand his *kibanja* using high-quality seedlings had no alternative but to adopt the modern farming. Unless he adopted the recommendations for spacing, hole-digging, and mixing the topsoil with manure, he could not obtain the seedlings from the BCU nurseries.

Establishment costs
for one acre (0.4 ha)

How could the costs of one acre or less of a Demonstration Plot come to shs 4 000/– within the first two years? The following table (22) deals with the establishment costs for one acre of modern bananas. The list of items and the figures in column 3 are quoted from Ngeze (1968) and the rest of the cost columns are calculated from the authors' Ihangiro survey. Ngeze reckons with 302 holes and suckers of bananas per acre, whereas the authors have applied 300 holes or suckers per acre, which accounts for the small and insignificant difference between the prices of some items.

The left part of the table shows a capital-intensive establishment of one acre, using entirely employed labour for all activities. The right part of the table shows a combination farm management, made up of employed labour and family labour force, and includes two different land-use types. Finally, the last column shows a farmer with his own manure supply.

The table is computed for pure establishing costs, regardless of any calculations of returns (these will be dealt with in Chapter 7). The main idea is to look at the various possibilities from a farmer's point of view, to show how different farmers can accommodate themselves according to their financial position and the availability of labour, and thus to demonstrate that a great deal of capital is not required to expand if enough family labour is available, assuming that the opportunity costs of family labour are equal to zero. The main capital inputs can be confined to grass and manure.

Cultivation

It is assumed that the *rweya* land is covered with a vegetation of small bush which must first be cut down, after which the stumps and tree roots must be removed

before the tractor can do the first ploughing. The tractor breaks the soil and turns over the sod, but as couch grass is common in Bukoba District, the acre has to be hoed very carefully throughout to remove the couch grass. This accounts for the many man-days spent on the second cultivation. If the first cultivation is done by hand, the main part of the couch grass will be removed during the first hoeing. This will take about one month if a person works very hard at a rate of 5 hours per day. The first hoeing is so exhausting that a person can usually work effectively for only 4 hours per day, finishing about 25 m² per day. The advantage of using the tractor is twofold: the cultivation work is shortened by 83 man-days, releasing the workers from the most exhausting work: and the cultivation costs are cut by around shs 100/–. It should be noted, however, that only the very few rich farmers are able to organize the tractor service, and the tractor service applied to scattered individual farming will mainly be a loss to the tractor agency.[12]

The advantage of working on formerly cultivated land (*ekishambu*) can be seen by comparing columns 5/6 with 7/8. According to the time the plot has been lying unmaintained, labour input for cultivation differs. The advantage of using *ekishambu* land comes primarily in the planting stage, where input of manure and grass can be reduced because of the greater content of humus in this soil and the better structure.

Those farmers using both hired labour and family labour will normally only expand ¼ to ½ an acre per year. The expansion ratio will be analysed at the end of the present chapter.

Digging holes

According to the supply and demand of labour force, the pay range for digging holes varies from –/40 c to –/10 c; coffee holes being smaller than banana holes, they are dug at a price from –/20 c to –/10 c.

Manure

In 1968 farmers paid –/50 c per *debe* of manure (FYM=farmyard manure). Where manure is scarce the price has gone up to 1/– per *debe* in 1970. When starting a banana plot on *rweya* land, farmers prefer to use 4 *debe* or more per banana hole for planting, whereas on better soil 2 *debe* are sufficient. The value of manure has long been known to the farmers, but the proper mixing of topsoil and manure in the planting hole, followed by a thick mulching, has speeded up the growth and flowering of both bananas and coffee. Formerly, the cooking bananas (*ebitoke*) took 24–28

Table 22. *Establishment costs (shs) for one acre (0.4 ha) of modern banana cultivation (Ukulima wa kisasa) at different labour wage rates. Ihangiro Division 1968*
A=man-days, B=wage rate/day

Items	Tractor & hired labour Rweya land No cattle				Hired & family labour Rweya land No cattle		Ekishambu No cattle		Cattle
	A	B 2/–	B 3/–[a]	B 4/60[f]	A	B 2/–	A	B 2/–	B 2/–
	(1)	(2)	(3)	(4)	(5)	(6)	(7)	(8)	(9)
1. Land clearing	40	80	120	184	40	80	30	60	60
2a. Ploughing tractor		70	70	70					
b. First cultivation hoe					160	320	124	248	248
3. Second cultivation hoe. Levelling land	133	266	400	612	56	112	56	112	112
Total cultivation	173	416	590	866	256	512	210	420	420
4. Digging holes @ –/40 c per hole		120	120/80	120		120		120	120
5. Manure:									
a. Cost FYM[b]		600	362/40	600		600		300[c]	
b. Manuring	20	40	60/40	92					
6. Planting:									
a. Cost of suckers @ –/50 c each		150	150	150					
b. Planting @ –/10 c per planted sucker		30	30/20	30					
7. Insecticides: Dieldrin against weevil		50	50	50		50		50	50
8. Mulching:									
a. Cost of grass[d]		400	500	400		400		200[e]	200
b. Spreading grass	30	60	90	138					
Total establishment		1 886	1 953/80	2 446		1 682		1 090	790

[a] P. B. N. M. Ngeze: "Report on an Appraisal of the Economies of Banana Growing as compared to Coffee and Tea in the Bukoba District." (Makerere University College, Kampala, 1968.)

[b] For *rweya* soil, farmers usually use 4 *debe* of manure per hole; price per *debe* in most areas is –/50 c (Column 3=–/30 c per *debe*).

[c] On *ekishambu* land which has formerly been cultivated with perennial crops farmers use 2 *debe* of manure per hole.

[d] Grass cut on the *rweya* land is bought in bundles. One bundle has an average weight of 20 kg and the farmers pay –/50 c per bundle. Price per bundle can go up to 1/– and down to –/20 c, according to the distance the grasscutter must transport the bundles. Grass-cutting is mainly done by Burundi workers or by women, and a woman can cut 3–4 bundles a day, which gives an income of shs 2/– per day.

Farmers mainly use 400 bundles per acre, but for establishing a modern acre on poor *rweya* soil, a progressive farmer will apply 800 bundles the first time and then continue with 400 bundles either every half year or every year.

[e] 400 bundles @ –/50 cents.

[f] BCU establishing labour pay-rate.

months to bear the first crop, and the later suckers 13–15 months.[13] Coffee was formerly expected to come into bearing after 6–8 years. Under modern husbandry the trees bear a fairly good crop after 3–4 years.[14]

The heavy application of cattle manure in modern farming increased the demand for this item, and the extension service therefore simultaneously had a campaign to teach the farmers to prepare compost, which again involved a considerable amount of extra work.

Planting

If a smallholder expands in the modern way at a rate of ¼ to ½ an acre, he will normally get his supply of suckers from his own *kibanja* or from those of his friends or relatives, according to the system of mutual help or customary *ujamaa*. Bananas are such an integrated part of Bahaya life that only 10–20 years ago it was unthinkable that anyone could charge a person for a sucker or refuse a relative or a friend permission to take some suckers for personal use.

If BCU or large entrepreneurs go into banana cultivation as an export crop, they must buy suckers, as they are outside the general social structure of Haya society. Furthermore, they must select special varieties to get a rather homogeneous population of high-yielding banana plants. In this case the price per sucker varies from –/10 c to –/50 c.

Transport costs

In Table 22 no transport costs for manure, suckers and grass bundles are given. Transport costs for the above-mentioned items are difficult to calculate unless lorry transport is involved, because the farmers gradually collect their items daily with the help of friends and relatives. This kind of transport, although it is considered as work by the farmers, is not regarded as capital investment, precisely as the utilization of family labour in peasant production is not counted in monetary terms or with any strict measurements.

Taking the wage rate of shs 4/60 a day, which can be used as BCU standard labour pay-rate, total costs for planting one acre are shs 2 446/–. To this amount transport costs should be added, so that total costs will rise above shs 3 000/– per acre. Then come labour costs for weeding, pruning and spraying, including second-year mulching with grass. It is not astonishing that the Demonstration Plot establishment costs for the first two years are estimated to be around shs 4 000/– per acre.

Ngeze, op.cit., cites the example of a man five miles from Bukoba town, who used coffee husk instead of manure. The husk was obtained from BUKOP Factory free of charge; he only had to pay the transport cost. The establishing cost amounted to shs 3 660/– for an acre. The different costs of items are shown in Table 23. The person in question used a spacing of 15′ by 15′, which gives 260 stools of banana per acre.

It is reasonable to assume that this man is either a BCU or a Government official or an M.P., so that he must pay the Government rate of 4/60 a day for wages. Nevertheless, his costs are shs 1 014/– more than the costs given in Column 4 in Table 22. He used an additional shs 400/– per bundle (being near the town: grass is scarce in the densely populated area; furthermore, the Bukoba Tea Estate is a large buyer of grass bundles at 1/– per bundle), or the table shows his costs for the first-year mulching twice. This may be the case; if so, his extra labour cost of shs 564/– can then account for maintenance, weeding and spreading grass the second time.

Comparing Tables 22 and 23, the establishing costs on *rweya* land range from shs 1 682/– (if the farmer has free manure supply at a value of 1 082/–) to shs 3 460/– for one acre of bananas.[15] The costs for establishing one acre of modern coffee cultivation are slightly lower, some 300 to 400 shillings less per acre.

From Table 22 it can be seen how farmers can accommodate according to the economy scale they can afford to use. In establishing a piece of *kibanja* in the modern style, there are three items to be considered by the farmers: labour, grass and manure.

Labour

Table 22 shows that labour is not a major bottleneck in the present system, because labour is available at a cheap rate at village level (shs 1/50 to 2/– per day).[16] The 2/– rate per man-day, which is applied as the general payment rate in Table 22, needs some comment. Farmers pay their employed labour either in kind (mainly bananas) or in cash, and throughout our sample the payment in kind showed an adjustment to the 2/– value, with some modification according to geographical location, either in relation to Bukoba town or to the distance to certain items. Table 24 gives the variation in values of different activities and items both in cash and in kind.

Piecework or contract work is very common, and several activities are nearly always done as piecework, such as the above-mentioned hole-digging, cutting grass bundles and picking coffee. That is why these activities are calculated at the same amount in the various columns of Table 22. Larger jobs such as land clearing will also usually be done on a piece-work basis

Table 23. *Establishment cost (shs) for one acre of bananas in modern style 5 miles outside Bukoba town on Rweya land*

1. Tractor to cultivate 1 acre twice	120
2. 9 labourers at shs 90/– each, plus one headman at shs 130/–	940
3. 15 lorries of husk at shs 50/–	750
4. Grass and mulching	800
5. Dieldrin	50
6. Miscellaneous work by labourers	800
Total	3 460

to speed up the work or if labour is scarce in peak seasons.

Grass

Tables 22 and 23 show that grass bundles for mulching the *kibanja* plot can exceed the investment costs of manure. Furthermore, if the farmer must obtain his supply of grass through the work of his family, considerable time must be set aside for this item, as it will take one person 80 to 100 man-days to cut the 400 bundles necessary for one acre. A good large bundle of *Hyparrhenia* grass weighs 20–25 kg, which means that only one bundle can be transported from the *rweya* to the village at a time by one person.

Manure

The value and importance of manure (FYM) have been stressed throughout this book; the supply of sufficient manure is a major bottleneck.[17] Compost manure was prepared by 12 per cent of the farmers[18] in the sample, and only one of the random-sample farmers used fertilizer, together with only a few rich farmers.

The problem of increasing the manure supply is not simply a matter of importing more cattle into the District. An increase in the cattle population will increase the strain on the *rweya* land, which within the present ecological system is the only source of grazing. At the same time the *rweya* land is the area for expansion of new *kibanja,* the supply source for the increased demand for mulching grass, and the area for *omusiri* cultivation.

The ecological balance between the two main land-use types, *kibanja* and *rweya,* cannot be maintained with both an increasing population and an increasing number of cattle. A change in animal husbandry (as mentioned on page 53) could enable an adjustment for the pressure on environmental resources. A change in the crop cultivation towards more intensive methods is already taking place, but so far this intensification is not an adjustment to the population increase, as it has been combined with an area expansion of the *kibanja* land-use type.

The large and 'rich' farmers have benefited from this approach of capital-intensive improvement methods because of the prevailing socio-economic system, with a stratification of the society into employers and employees, the loopholes in the coffee trading and marketing system, and the organization of the credit and loan system.

Table 24. *Variation in payment of employed labour 1968–1969*

Activities	Shillings Daily	Range Monthly	Kind: Bunches of bananas
All types of farm work	2/–	45/–, 50/–	1 bunch a day
Clearing land	1/50, 2/–		1 bunch a day (6 hrs)
One hole, banana	–/40		1 bunch = 5 holes
One hole, banana	–/20		1 bunch = 10 holes
One hole, banana	–/10		1 bunch = 20 holes
One hole, coffee	–/10		1 bunch = 20 holes
One grass bundle	1/–		1 bunch = 2 bundles
One grass bundle	–/50		1 bunch = 4 bundles
One grass bundle	–/20		1 bunch = 10 bundles
Mulching	2/–	45/– variation 30/– to 50/–	1 bunch per day
Weeding	1/50 4 hrs	35/– to 45/– (usually)	Size differs according to hours
	2/– 6 hrs		
Picking coffee	1/– per *debe* fresh coffee		
Processing beer	5/– a day		
Processing coffee	3/– a day		

Credit and Loan System

Under the BCU credit system two main types of agricultural loans are available to those farmers who are members of a BCU primary society.

1. *Emergency loans.* These loans can be obtained at no interest on a short-term basis not exceeding six months. The period for acquiring the loan is between the first and the last payments for the coffee. The loans are paid out of the reserve funds of the society and are deducted from the final payment to the individual farmer. This means that the size of the loan is directly related to the number of kilos of coffee delivered to the society by the individual farmer. The farmer can receive 10 cents per kilo for *maganda* (unhulled coffee) and 20 cents per kilo for FAQ (hulled and clean coffee) (1970).

The decision about who is to receive emergency loans is made by the committee of the primary society; the loan conditions as well as the entire socio-economic pattern of the rural society favour the coffee traders and the rural elite. No specific conditions are attached to these loans.

The emergency loans were originally initiated in 1956 to help farmers with school fees, payment of hospital treatment, food purchase, etc. In fact, the loans could be used for whatever the farmers needed, and the main concern of the BCU was to get its money back.

2. *The rehabilitation loans.* These loans are financed by the NDCA (National Development Credit Agency) and were set up in 1966. The farmers apply to their primary society for a loan to be used for improved farming. E.g., the farmer who is uprooting his old coffee trees and replacing them with new coffee seedlings in the modern way (*ukulima wa kisasa*) needs the money to pay for grass mulch, manure, spraying or pruning equipment after he has begun rehabilitation. The agricultural Field Assistant Officer (*Bwana Shamba*) then visits the farmer and thereafter advises the Committee of the primary society, which on this basis decides whether the farmer should be granted a loan, if the funds are made available. All the applications are forwarded to the BCU.

The BCU applies to the NDCA, which grants the fund at an interest rate of $7\frac{1}{2}$ per cent and the same interest is charged by the BCU on the loans to the farmers. The BCU is responsible for the repayment to the NDCA via the repayment from the primary societies. The repayment period varies with the terms of the loan made by the NDCA to the BCU.

The size of the funds and the terms have been as follows:

1966—total loan of shs 500 000 repayable in 3 years
1967—total loan of shs 1 000 000 repayable in 5 years
1968—total loan of shs 1 000 000 repayable in 7 years
1969—total loan of shs 800 000 repayable in 7 years.
For 1968 and 1969 the period of grace has been two
    years. The amount of the loan granted to the farmer
    depends on a three-year average value of the farm-
    er's coffee delivery.

Formerly the evaluation of the farmers' agricultural husbandry was done by the Kilimo (Ministry of Agriculture, Food and Co-operatives) *Bwana Shamba*. After most of these were posted to *Ujamaa* Villages in 1968, the BCU has trained its own *Bwana Shambas*, called "Agricultural Auxiliaries". These 74 persons, one for each of the primary societies in the West Lake Region, are mainly people who have been working for the Union in its spraying and pruning teams. They have undergone 3 weeks' training in extension techniques and advising on rehabilitation loans.

3. *Cattle loans.* Early in 1971 NDCA[19] gave the BCU approval to give cattle loans to members for purchasing heifers, which the BCU imports from Musoma. In April 1971 300 heifers arrived from Musoma. The amount of the loan will cover the cost of the animal. An upper limit of no more than 3 animals per member is set by the Union. Repayment is over 4 years, with a one-year period of grace.

According to the Manager of the BCU, the distribution of the loans should be to poorer farmers, regardless of coffee deliveries, as the loans can be secured against the cattle and their offspring. The key personnel in allocating the loans are still the *Bwana Shamba* and the Committee members of the Primary Society.

4. *Tea loans.* Farmers joining the smallholder tea scheme around the Bukoba Tea Estate are given fertilizer and tea stumps on credit. The loan is deducted from their payments for their deliveries of tea leaves and as these deliveries are spread out over the whole year the repayment is not felt as much as those for the coffee loans. The tea loans are the loans best geared towards agricultural development. The BCU's role here has been as financier.

Impact of the Extension Service

The effort made since 1965 to convince farmers of the economic benefits of modern farming methods has two aspects: 1. The impact on the peasant society; i.e., the degree to which the peasants responded to the innovations. 2. Were all peasants able to apply the benefits of modern farming? Or had the whole extension programme some built-in factors which biased the development in favour of a certain group of peasants?

Table 25 indicates that the response to the extension campaign since 1965 has been positive and half of even the very small farmers use manure and grass, the main items of improvement, to get a better yield. According to the slow expansion rate for smallholders (see Table 19, page 60) these farmers are able to cover a major part of their manure demand through family/friend relationships, whereas grass, especially in areas with land shortage (Kanyigo) must be bought with cash.

The use of fertilizer as a substitute for FYM or compost has not penetrated the peasant society at all. Of the 18 'rich' farmers only 4 have used fertilizer and in very insignificant quantities (1–3 bags per year) and of the random-sample farmers, virtually none.

Spraying is progressing slowly and the Kanyigo area with its very small *kibanja* plots has reacted most positively, as it can be more fatal to lose the coffee production from a very small farm unit. This might also be due to the higher level of education or the longer tradition of education.

No table has been computed for the rich farmers, as it is implicit in the definition that those farmers have responded to the extension campaign, except for fertilizer application.

One should conclude that the extension campaign for husbandry improvement has been a success, especially when the former resistance is borne in mind, and considering also the short period of time, five years. Only the improvement of harvesting techniques, drying and processing has not been successful, mainly due to the inability of the BCU to reward the farmers who do produce high-quality coffee with a better price.

The economic benefits of modern farming

There are three main incentives to respond positively to improved crop husbandry on the modern lines:

1. Expectation of a higher yield per unit area
2. Expectation of a better price for a better quality of product
3. Access to credit facilities if a farmer applies modern farming, as modern farming needs capital investment.

As incentive no. 2 has not hitherto been fulfilled, farmers have concentrated on output expansion, mainly combined with an area expansion of farm units. Farm unit expansion on a large scale (=1–2 acres, 0.4–0.8 ha per year) can only be done by farmers with some capital available either in the form of large *kibanja* units or from income sources outside agriculture. As these two factors are interdependent, it is understandable that only the so-called rich farmers have been able to expand on a large scale. Furthermore, the loan and credit facilities have been allocated on a calculation of a three-year output basis for the farmers' production of coffee, to assure that the farmers can repay both the loan and the interest. This again was in favour of the rich farmers, but unfortunately also in favour of the coffee traders, some of them having very small farm units which do not allow for large deliveries to the primary societies, but who have nevertheless been able to obtain loans from societies for 'agricultural improvement' on the basis of their pounds of coffee delivered.

One side effect of the modernization programme is

Table 25. *Percentage of farmers in random sample responding to extension service. 1969–1970 season*

	Ibwera	Nshamba	Kanyigo
1. Using manure for planting coffee or bananas[a]	55	50	70
1 a. Of these farmers, those buying manure:	15	30	25
2. Using fertilizer	–	–	5
3. Spraying coffee	10	10	20
4. Insecticides for bananas	5	–	10 (60)[b]
5. Using grass mulch	44	50	55[c]
5a. Of these farmers those buying grass bundles	25	34	40

[a] The percentage does not indicate that all these farmers planted in the modern way (see Table 21, page 61). Some of them merely planted 5–10 coffee trees or banana plants within their traditional *kibanja*.
[b] During a heavy attack of banana weevil, BCU supplied insecticides 'free of charge' and during that time 60% of the farmers applied insecticides. When the free supply stopped the percentage dropped to 10%.
[c] 30% of the Kanyigo farmers have expanded in modern farming, but 55% were buying grass bundles, as some farmers apply grass mulch to their traditional *kibanja*.

the uprooting of coffee trees, replacing them with bananas. This applies to farmers near Bukoba town or farmers with transport facilities or easy access to main roads. Bananas have so far been competitive with coffee, so long as the inland market is not saturated. The majority of peasants in Bukoba District will nevertheless continue to depend on coffee as the main cash crop, even though diversification to tea growing and ranching is increasing.

The role of BCU in the political-economic pattern

From the survey it can be concluded that less than 10 per cent of the peasants in Bukoba District are among the rich farmers, in the sense that they have been able to attain rapid economic development through modern farming, and a majority of this 10 per cent already belonged to the privileged class of the population before modern farming was introduced.

The BCU Demonstration Plots, Extension Service and loans have made a significant impact on the peasants' attitude towards more intensive farming methods, supported by extension work done by the agricultural extension staff from the Ministry of Agriculture. It must be remembered that the economic organization of the Union was established during British rule, the top officials of the Union were trained in Western countries, the independence of Tanzania did not bring any immediate change in the economic institutions of the Region, and that the BCU within the acknowledged capitalistic socio-economic pattern of Buhaya has been a very successful enterprise.

It should further be remembered that although the Arusha Declaration came in early 1967 and the President's 'Ujamaa Vijijini' was published in September 1967, the idea of transforming the rural society according to the Nation's socialist objectives first really started to penetrate the local administration with the coming of the Presidential circular of 23 March 1969. The Union has until 1971 had no direct political influence, but of course a major influence indirectly, as many of the rich farmers benefiting from modern farming and credit facilities have been people with political influence. A radical change in political ideology, and hence the implementation of this ideology through economic institutions requires some time for adjustment.

Notes

1. For a detailed analysis of the pre-independence agricultural policy see Austen, R. A., *Northwest Tanzania under German and British Rule*, Yale University Press 1968; Hydén, G., *Political Development in Rural Tanzania*, E. African Publ. House, Nairobi 1969; Mukurasi, P. W., *The Bukoba Co-operative Union as an Instrument of Agricultural Innovation*, Political Science—Paper 7: Dissertation, University College, Dar es Salaam 1970.
2. It is a tradition to leave about two metres of the stem after cutting down the banana bunch. This part is considered to be the "mother" for the new sucker (the "child", in Kihaya called *omwana gw'engemu.)* Thus the old mother stem contains a lot of juice, and the child has to suck from the mother to be healthy (personal communication with farmers). When the piece of the mother stem has dried up and started to rot it is uprooted and spread on the ground as mulch.
3. P. de Schlippe, *Shifting Cultivation in Africa*, London, 1956: "In some other cases, far-reaching agrarian reforms are undertaken based on extremely sound ideas, but they fail because of the lack of knowledge of some details unimportant to our minds, but all-important to the cultivator, and not only to him but to his natural environment." (p. xi)
4. In 1946 the Bukoba Native Coffee Board took over the marketing function, in order to break the monopoly of the Indian coffee dealers and to provide for a greater surplus for the farmers, by introducing a second payment.
5. Bukoba Native Co-operative Union Ltd.: *Report for the years 1961–1964*.
6. BNCU *Report*, p. 9: "Though well sprayed, the old coffee trees did not make a good yield and more often many turned out barren. It was therefore, imperative for the Union to launch pruning cam-

paigns."—This implies that some of the trees in Columns 1 and 3 are the same, first sprayed and then pruned [authors' comment].
7. The seedlings were not really free of charge; the farmers paid for them through their coffee, as BNCU charged a certain levy on the coffee to cover the cost of the seedlings.
8. The field staff within the Ministry of Agriculture and Co-operatives, Agricultural Division for Bukoba District, was in 1967 forty-one, of whom twenty-four were Assistant Field Officers and fifteen Field Assistants, with circa 35 of them permanently in the field, in an area with about 103 000 rural households, which gives a ratio of *one* extension officer to *3 000* households.
9. With the modern spacing, one acre of bananas contains 300 clumps of bananas, and one acre of coffee 540 trees (=750 bananas and 1 350 coffee trees per hectare).
10. Mukurasi, op. cit. page 44: "We can therefore conclude, that the Union has proved that the farmer, with the right grassroot approach on the part of the agencies of agricultural innovation, has the ability and the will to change his farming ways but only if *the necessary capital inputs* are within his reach and also if the forms of investment have got some economic payoffs."
West Lake Annual Report 1968: "Weeding and mulching were nicely performed though some farmers were not able to do so due to lack of funds."
11. It also applies to farmers in Kyamtwara and Kianja Divisions located near the market in Bukoba town.
12. The main agency for tractor service is BCU Ltd. BCU was given 19 tractors in 1964 by the Government in the form of a loan, installments of which were payable yearly for a five-year period. The tractors were mainly allocated for large-scale operations of tea, sugar canes and cotton, but they have also been hired out to individual farmers. "From 1964 the time when the Union received the tractors, up to the end of 1967/68, the loss amounted to shs 1 036, 878/-." (BCU *Report 1965/65–1967/68*). In 1971 most of the tractors had been sold, and no individual farmers can rent tractor service.
13. J. S. Ishengoma, *Rweya Land Cultivation II*, Maruku District Book 1956: "Where no cattle is owned and nothing in the form of manure is added to the soil, the boiling types will take 24–28 months . . ."
14. District Agricultural Officer, personal communication.
15. This is still seen from the farmer's point of view, and no calculation is made concerning the value of cattle.
16. The rate of shs 1/50 to 2/– applies to labourers coming from outside Bukoba; i.e., Ruanda/Burundi migrant labour normally coming in for half-year periods. It would be difficult to get the Bahaya themselves to work for this rate of pay.
17. "Unavailability of manure in the planting holes was the major problem which accounted for fewer seedlings planted during the planting season. Efforts were made to encourage farmers to prepare compost heaps thus to get sufficient manure for planting, but though there was some response, the compost prepared was not sufficient to fill the planting holes.

The use of coffee husk was also made but because many farmers could not obtain it from its sources, due to transport facilities and inadequacy of the husk the problems of manure could not be lifted." (West Lake *Annual Report*, Min. of Agr., 1968.)
18. ⅜ of the farmers making compost were from Ibwera, where only 15 per cent of the farmers own cattle.
19. The activities of the NDCA have been concluded and its credits and liabilities transferred to the Rural Development Bank.

Chapter 6. The Ihangiro Time Study

In the previous chapters we have described the physical resources of Bukoba District, their potential and constraints. In a spatial context we have analysed the land-use pattern and we have shown the importance of *kibanja* land within the land tenure system. Furthermore, we have argued that the extension advice offered by Kilimo and the BCU has been adopted mainly by a minority of farmers, the so-called "rich farmers", while the loan facilities and the change in land tenure to individual ownership as well as the whole set-up of the coffee economy have created a "rural elite" of farmers. The term "rural elite" applies to the capitalistic framework of the Haya society. Within the *ujamaa* framework of today's Tanzania, members of this stratum should be termed "kulaks" or "petty-capitalists". This minority has developed much quicker than the majority of small holders in Bukoba District.

We now intend to analyse the labour resources through a very detailed survey of 31 selected farmers in one division of the District. We have chosen Ihangiro Division for our sample because we lived there for nearly two years and had the kind of contact with the farmers which is necessary for a detailed socio-economic study. One objective was that the farmers participating in the survey should receive an immediate benefit from their co-operation, i.e., the surveyors and the farmers should learn from each other and have a constant dialogue about the objectives of the work.

The input or use of time was, however, not confined to agricultural work, as we wanted to look at the rural society as a totality, where the different ways of using time or allocating manpower are equally important in understanding the social structure of the peasant village life.

We were interested in the role of men and women in the peasant society, because we met contradictory statements and prejudices, such as: "Bahayas are lazy; they do not like to work but employ labourers. The women do most of the agricultural work and the men especially are more interested in leisure and drinking than in improved standards of living;" "The Bahaya men do most of the agricultural work; when they can see a profit, they work very hard and they easily adopt new crops and cultivation techniques." Therefore we shall first give some quantitative data on how adult men and women use their time during a 12-hour day throughout the year; next, we shall look at the allocation of labour on different crops and activities throughout the year.

Composition of labour force in the time study sample

To examine the allocation of labour we made a study of how people spent their time throughout the year 1969 in Ihangiro. In the study 269 persons were recorded on 31 farm units. Originally 32 farmers were selected, but one farmer was imprisoned for 5 months and was therefore excluded during the final processing. The farmers were selected to be representative of the distribution of farm size in the main random sample in the division, and at the same time such that two modes of farm production should also be represented. These two modes were (1) the farm unit worked only by family labour, including visiting friends in the traditional context of *ujamaa*, and (2) the farm unit worked by the family labour force and employed labourers. Half of the men in the study were part-time farmers, the other half full-time farmers.

Daylight activities

Bukoba District is situated between latitudes 1°0′ and 2°15′ south of the Equator. Therefore, it very conveniently made sense to use a 12-hour day for measuring the daylight activities. Records were kept from 7 a.m. until 7 p.m. and the daylight activities were divided into 5 major groups: 1) *Agricultural work,* 2) *Employment or business* outside the farm unit, 3) *Social activities,* 4) *Domestic work*—this included all work related to activities in and around the house, such as fetching water and firewood, cooking and washing, housebuilding and repairs, eating, brewing pombe, fetching food from the plots, etc.; for convenience' sake, it also included animal husbandry for the five farmers owning cattle, 5) *Leisure*—everything coming

Table 26. *Age and sex distribution of labour force in the time study sample*

	Age	Number		Total
Permanent members of household working on the farm unit				
Male adults (husbands)	21–65	29		
Female adults (wives)	18–65	34		
Female adults (mothers)	45–65	6		
		69		69
		Not at school	At school	
Male children	7–20	14	19	
Female children	7–25	17	17	
Male relatives	7–45	4	4	
Female relatives	7–45	11	2	
		46	42	88
Permanently employed males	20–50	3		3
Total persons living permanently in the household and working on farm unit				160
Persons temporarily working on the farm unit				
Male employed labourers		36		
Female employed labourers		16		
		52		52
Visiting relatives, friends, neighbours and *ujamaa* groups	57–90[a]			57
Total temporary workers				109
Grand total				269

[a] The visiting group of people were difficult to classify. The 57 persons did more than one day's work, while the 33 others merely helped a few hours during a visit. Many people appeared several times on the record sheets, so that the figures give an estimated range of the number of visitors during the year who do some work on the farm. A proper record was kept of how many man-hours they contributed, but no attempt was made to keep a separate record for each person.

under the two Swahili terms *kupumzika* (to rest) and *kutembea* (to take a walk and go around and meet people). We must admit that it is not satisfactory to include *kutembea* as "leisure", as this term also can cover productive work. When you walk around in the village, many important decisions can be made concerning your social and economic life, and as such it is very productive. Many of these decisions belong to the secrets of a person's life or between two persons and there was, of course, no possibility of recording them.

First, we shall compare the main daylight activities for adult women and men, dividing the men into full-time farmers and part-time farmers with employment or other work outside the farm unit. Then we shall give two case studies to show the variation in the distribution within separate farm units.

Distribution of daylight activities (1969)

In Diagrams 13 and 14 and in Table 27, average figures for the 3 groups of adults in the Ihangiro peasant society have been used to show the general trend in the allocation of people's time on the main activities during the year. The percentages have been computed from the actual hours people spent per month on the different activities.

Diagram 13 gives an overall view of the distribution of activities. The different columns indicate for each month the percentage of the time available (in a 12-hour day) which is used for the different activities. For each diagram the percentage for the whole year for each activity is written on the shading.

A major viewpoint adopted here is that when we look at adult people's life as an entirety, all kinds of work, whether agricultural, domestic, or related to social obligations, are considered as *productive* work, as opposed to leisure. This means that for the daylight activities even taking a meal or staying in a hospital is considered as work.

In Table 27, below, the major trends are summarized. Among the people relying only on farming for their living, the women do more agricultural and domestic work than the men (on the average, 14 per cent more).

The total work (71 per cent) for women (Class A) amounts to 3 110 hours per year, which corresponds to 8½ hours per day. Full-time farmers, i.e., men (class B)

Table 27. *General trends in distribution of daylight activities, percentage of the year*

	Full-time in agriculture		Part-time in agriculture
	A Women	B Men	C Men
Agricultural and domestic work	59	45	26
Social work	12	11	15
Employment or business			25
Total work	71	56	66
Leisure	29	44	34
Total activities	100	100	100

use 2 427 hours per year for the various work activities, equivalent to 6½ hours per day, and part-time farmers, i.e., men (Class C) 2 886 hours, which corresponds to nearly 8 hours per day. As the recording only went up to 7 p.m. every day, 1 or 1½ hours can be added to the women's work, accounting for the evening meal preparation, etc., thus giving the women a minimum working day of 9–10 hours.

Looking at the Haya peasant society as a whole at its present stage of development and social organization, two groups of adults (Class A and C) are occupied with productive activities for two-thirds of their time, while the third group, full-time farmers (men), are favoured in being occupied for only about half of their time.

Thus, Diagram 13 tells us that if one wants to think of development in terms of increased work input in the agricultural sector, classes A and C of the adults have no spare time available, whereas Class B men could increase their labour input by about 10 per cent. Therefore, an increase in labour input can—except in the case of male full-time farmers—only be obtained by reducing the time spent on the other activities mentioned above. Since the majority of farmers have access only to labour-intensive inputs, not to capital-intensive ones, increased input thus requires the reallocation of the use of time and a consequent change in social structure and values.

To facilitate comparison, the four main activities in Diagram 13 are shown separately in Diagram 14, each drawn up with the same base line. As we compare the three classes of adults, we shall describe the content of the activities.

Agricultural work

Agricultural work, which accounts for one-fourth of the women's time and one-fifth of the time of full-time male farmers, includes all work in the field, hulling of the dried coffee cherries, threshing of beans and the hours spent walking to distant plots. (For further analysis see the next section, on agricultural activities.)

Looking at the three agricultural diagrams 14 A, B, C, the noticeable feature is the lack of peaks in labour input. The small peak of 35 per cent for the women in January accounts for 4.2 hours per day. If the labour input is calculated on the basis of actual working days (250 working days a year; see page 78), the daily labour input for women can reach 6 hours for agricultural field work in January and February.

Class C farmers for six months of the year spend less than one hour per day in agricultural work, as they are occupied with work outside their farm unit for one-fourth of their time (Employment-graph). These part-time farmers include all kinds of local craftsmen: carpenters, bricklayers, local building constructors, timber sawers, tailors, hairdressers and skilled casual labourers; businessmen such as coffee-traders, bar-owners, pombe-brewers, and one clerk.

These farmers either replace their own work by employed labour as long as they can obtain cheap labourers from Burundi or they keep their farm unit at a size which can be run by the family labour force. The variations in the business pattern are manifold. One man has a contract with a neighbouring estate to provide grass mulch for the coffee fields; he hires Burundi labourers to cut the grass and is himself a manager. Another has a contract with a trader who supplies bananas to the Mwanza market: he buys up bananas in the villages and sells them to the trader. A third expands his farm unit through capital input obtained from trading in coffee.

The agricultural diagrams only show the average allocation of time for women and men, respectively. For the case studies of the individual farmer, the monthly fluctuation is wider (see Diagrams 15 and 16) and it must be remembered that a substantial input comes from children, relatives and hired labour.

Domestic work

For all three classes of adults most work is concerned with activities centred around the house or on work concerned with improving the housing facilities. Of the total of 34 per cent of the women's time spent on domestic work, about 20 per cent is used for preparing food. In a farm economy where the bulk of the food comes from the farmer's own unit a great deal of time is used for fetching the food, cleaning it and preparing it. Firewood must be collected and cut, water fetched, etc. The fire must be maintained and controlled, while at the same time other activities can take place, such as drying coffee, shelling groundnuts, drying beans, etc.

The peak in July and August is due to the dry season in Ihangiro, where water must be brought from rivers. In 1969, Ihangiro did not receive a single drop of rain during those two months (see Rainfall, Diagram 7). At the end of the dry season some of the nearby streams may dry up, so that people must go further to obtain water, while the different streams and water-collecting points also differ in the quality of water. During the rainy season much time is saved by collecting water from the corrugated roof. (In June 1971 all farmers in

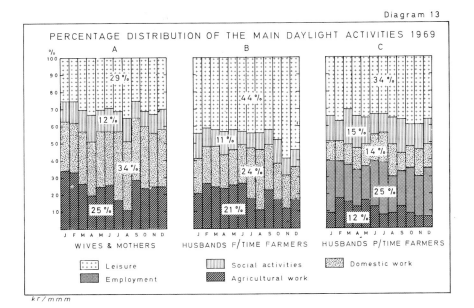

Diagram 13

PERCENTAGE DISTRIBUTION OF THE MAIN DAYLIGHT ACTIVITIES 1969

kr/mmm

the sample received piped water from collection points in the villages.) Also included in the domestic work diagram is washing clothes. Men and women usually take care of their own clothes and they go to special washing points by the streams. (See also Map 5.)

The mutual help in agricultural work exercised on other people's farm units, e.g., planting beans together, which is traditional *ujamaa* work done by groups of women, is included in the domestic classification. We wanted to keep labour input on the farmer's own unit separate, because animal husbandry is included in the domestic work of the class B and C farmers. This takes into account the fact that only about 3 per cent of the cattle-owners' time is spent on herding duty, while most of it is spent near the house milking the cows. Taking the cows to and from the *rweya* pasture is often a task done by children in the family.

The main activities for the full-time farmers are pombe-brewing and housebuilding or improvement of house facilities and the mutual help in these activities, as well as participation in hunting parties for vermin control.

Social activities

During the recording of the social activities, the recorders simply wrote down what people were doing, where they were going and for what reasons. During the processing of the data the social activities were divided into the following groups, listed here in order of priority for men and women.

Under the term "other social visits" are included all general kinds of visits through which a person maintains the social links with family members and friends, in order to maintain his reputation of being a good and respected person in the society, e.g., visiting parents, bringing beer to one's father-in-law, paying a visit when a child is born, taking some of the farm products to relatives, etc. These kinds of activities usually involve a safari outside the village, and preparation of the gifts to be brought. During these mutual visits an exchange (mainly of food products and beer) takes place. The visits, which are planned and expected, account for nearly 10 per cent of the woman's time and about 6 per cent of the full-time farmer's time. The part-time farmer must maintain a wider circle of acquaintances, owing to his specific business; his social obligations may also be greater if he is known to have a regular cash income.

Within the village many of these visits (especially to friends) take place during leisure hours and they are more improvised.

The activities take place throughout the year with no specific peak months. The two priority lists emphasize the importance of the social life within the family and clan and a circle of close friends; there is nothing remarkable about that. Four out of the first five priorities are identical for men and women. Nevertheless, men go more regularly to the market than women

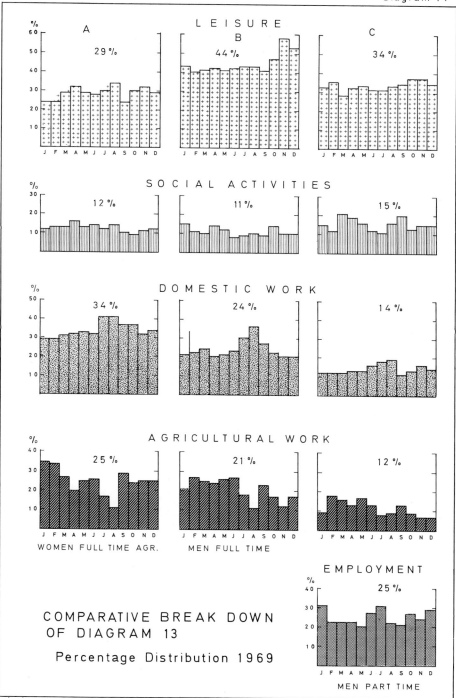

L E I S U R E

S O C I A L   A C T I V I T I E S

D O M E S T I C   W O R K

A G R I C U L T U R A L   W O R K

WOMEN FULL TIME AGR.   MEN FULL TIME

E M P L O Y M E N T

COMPARATIVE BREAK DOWN
OF DIAGRAM 13

Percentage Distribution 1969

MEN PART TIME

kr / m m m

74

Table 28. *Priority list for social activities for:*

All men	All women
1. Other social visits	1. Other social visits
2. Going to the market	2. Assistance during morning
3. Visits to sick relatives	3. Visits to sick relatives
4. Assistance during mourning	4. Hospital and dispensary
5. Religious and other festivals	5. Religious and other festivals
6. Meetings	6. Going to the market
7. Hospital and dispensary	7. Fetching medicine
8. Court cases	8. Meetings
9. Fetching medicine	9. Court cases

and for natural reasons women are more often admitted to the dispensary than men. As a whole it can be seen that men attend public functions more than women.

Leisure

The time spent in leisure is often taken as an indicator of laziness, and it is very often used as an explanation for the lack of development among smallholders in Bukoba. If one looks at the leisure diagram for the class B farmers, it seems to support this theory, but we nevertheless cannot accept this explanation, as life is much more complicated and does not allow for such generalizations. First we must ask: who are the persons making the statement about laziness? They are mainly the administrators and the well-off farmers, the

group we have called the rural elite. This group has managed to be released from hard manual work, because of capital available to employ labourers or to buy certain necessary inputs like grass and manure. Those are the people blaming the others for not liking to work hard with the hoe. It is, in short, hypocrisy.

Furthermore, the same group that has supported and promoted individualism in the peasant society, in the colonial system, and the post-independence administration has been unable to stop either coffee smuggling or coffee trading, the latter keeping the smallholders in a vicious circle of dependency. The leisure diagram for class B is not statistically significant, but it does give a hint; we must look for comparative data to assess whether men can work more in agriculture if the economic incentives are there (see page 90).

Two case studies of daylight activities

Before closing this section, two case studies, one a full-time farmer with 1.08 ha under cultivation and the other a part-time farmer with 3.51 ha under cultivation, are shown in Diagrams 15 and 16. This is done partly to illustrate how the average diagrams hide individual variations, but also to show that in spite of these variations, the trends are fairly constant, especially for agricultural and for leisure activities, with the major fluctuations occurring mainly within the domestic and social activity groups.

Farmer C   Diagram 15

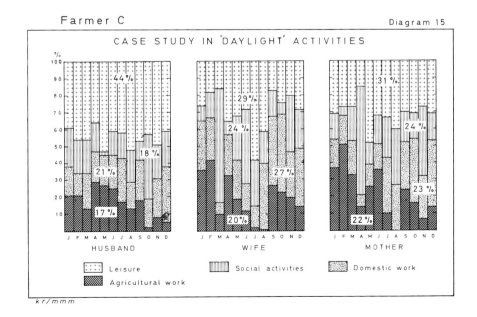

kr/mmm

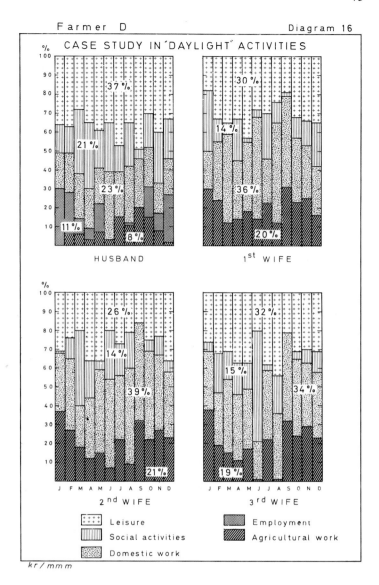

Farmer D   Diagram 16

CASE STUDY IN 'DAYLIGHT' ACTIVITIES

HUSBAND   1st WIFE

2nd WIFE   3rd WIFE

Leisure   Employment
Social activities   Agricultural work
Domestic work

kr/mmm

Diagram 15 shows a full-time farmer who runs his one-hectare farm unit with the help of his wife and his mother; for a few months he also had a divorced sister helping him. The peaks and troughs in the agricultural columns are more marked than on the average diagrams, while the proportion of the time used for agriculture remains roughly the same. The time spent in leisure is the same as the average figure, but the domestic and social activities fluctuate widely from the average.

When reading the diagram the following comments will throw light on the changes from month to month. The wife left for the main part of March and half of

June to take care of a sick relative in another village, while the mother was admitted for hospital treatment in April and had to help relatives in November because of a death.

The farm unit is small and therefore there is a marked decline in agricultural activity during the dry season, July and August, which is accentuated by the fact that this year was a bad year for coffee yield, so that the coffee harvest in May and June was quickly finished.

The women's agricultural work is divided between work in the *kibanja* (60 per cent) and work in *omusiri* (40 per cent). The permanent family labour force con-

76

Table 29. *Percentage distribution of time used on social activities for husbands from the two case studies in Diagrams 15 and 16*

Priority list of social activities	Husband's Diagram 15 (full-time farmers)	Husband's Diagram 16 (part-time farmers)
1. Other social visits	31.0	22.9
2. Going to the market	26.2	14.7
3. Visits to sick relatives	18.7	1.4
4. Assistance during mourning	11.2	2.5
5. Religious and other festivals	6.2	3.6[a]
6. Meetings	1.2	25.2
7. Hospital and dispensary	1.8	1.1
8. Court cases	–	26.1
9. Fetching medicine	3.7	2.5
Total	100	100

[a] The part-time farmer belongs to the Lutheran Church and has been put under church discipline because of his three wives.

sists of the three people in the diagram, but their work covers only 78 per cent of all field work done in the one-hectare farm unit. The remaining 22 per cent is done by relatives and friends.

Diagram 16 shows a part-time farmer with 3.5 ha, of which 0.4 ha is *omusiri,* mainly prepared and planted the previous year, which means that nearly all agricultural work is done in the *kibanja.* In addition to his three wives, the farmer has 7 children available for agricultural work, although 4 of them are in school, and during peak seasons he hires up to 10 labourers for coffee harvest and weeding activities. The man is merely a manager on his farm, a responsibility which he shares with his first wife, who is really in charge of the day-to-day work of the farm.

The husband's main activity in agriculture is pruning the coffee trees and the banana stems. His non-agricultural work is irregular, as it involves owning a share in a bar and making school dresses for a primary school.

The fact that 23 per cent of his time is used for domestic work is due to his animal husbandry: he milks his cows every day. His social activities also take a larger share of the total time than in the case of the average part-time farmer, since he is a village headman and has more obligations in the court and public meetings. Table 29 shows the percentage distribution of time used for social activities for the two husbands.

In the case of the full-time farmer the order of priorities is almost the same as the average pattern

listed on page 74, while the part-time farmer's public obligations are clearly displayed in the table.

The distribution of the activities of the three wives is fairly uniform and follows the average of Diagram 13 quite closely, although one-fifth of their time is spent in agricultural field work, which is a little less than the average figure. The third wife worked less than the other two, as she was pregnant and delivered a child in June. The peaks in domestic activities in September for all wives are due to the mutual help on other farm units for planting beans.

The four adults in diagram 16 do 40 per cent of the total agricultural work in the field. 29 per cent is done by the children living at home and relatives, and the remaining 31 per cent of the total input on this 3.5 ha farm unit is performed by hired labour.

Input of adult family labour in agricultural section. Division of labour between men and women

The farming system of Bukoba District consists of full-time farmers and part-time farmers operating a mixed farm economy of integrated animal husbandry and agriculture. The agricultural section has two main components, perennial crops and annual crops, related to two well-defined types of land use, the *kibanja* and the *omusiri.*

It has been shown how certain changes in the resources of the Haya economy have influenced land tenure, land use and cultivation techniques. These changes have taken a particular direction under the influence of the extension policy of Kilimo and the BCU.

The way the Bahaya allocate their labour force in the agricultural sector has also undergone changes. Before the introduction of the cash crop coffee, a clear division of labour between men and women was found, and even today some division can still be distinguished for certain activities, certain crops and their related land-use types.

Most of the part-time farmers are men, as employment opportunities for women outside the farm units are very limited. Nevertheless, if there is a demand for female labour, e.g., on the Bukoba Tea Estate, women may take up payed employment. In some cases they may also do piecework such as cutting grass for mulch.

For the full-time farmer a division of labour related to land-use types is found. In general *omusiri* work is performed only by women and *kibanja* work by both sexes. Within the traditional *kibanja* system men are in charge of the husbandry of the perennial crops bananas and coffee (with the exception of the harvesting of coffee, which is done by the whole family; the wife decides on the use of the food bananas, but the husband has the responsibility for the beer bananas). The interplanting of annual crops in the *kibanja* is done by women and children. Men are completely in charge of the animal husbandry, hunting vermin, building houses and brewing beer.

With the introduction of the more labour-intensive cultivation techniques of *kibanja* (*ukulima wa kisasa*), a gradual change in the division of labour is taking place and the working relationship between men and women is becoming more integrated. This is especially true in the case of young farmers.

An interesting example of how the diversification of the so-called traditional coffee/banana-*omusiri* system has influenced the division of agricultural labour between the sexes is found in the smallholder tea scheme outside Bukoba town (surveyed by A. A. Moody, 1970). Tea is a labour-demanding crop throughout the year, and if it is cultivated on a family-labour basis, the women must be involved in the plucking of the tea leaves. To adjust to this additional labour input (the tea farmers still maintain their *kibanja* with coffee and bananas) the women have given up part of their *omusiri* cultivation to participate in the much more profitable tea cultivation. (See comparision with Moody's data at the end of this chapter.)

In Table 30, below, an attempt is made to outline the division of labour still existing in the Ihangiro area.

Labour input by men and women related to land-use types

Diagram 17 shows the average monthly labour input in terms of working hours for men and women; that is, the recorded amount of hours used by both sexes in agricultural field work. The use of man-equivalents applied by Collinson and the researchers from the German IFO Institute[1] did not make sense in the Bukoba farming system, where the division of labour is related to different land-use types and crops and where the main agricultural activity, hand-weeding, can be done equally well by men, women and children.

The classes of adult farmers are the same as used in the diagrams for daylight activities. Here the labour input done by women is split up according to land-use

Table 30. *Division of labour between men and women in the agricultural sector*

(m or w)=men or women may participate now

Activity					
Coffee			*Bananas*		
Digging holes	m		Digging holes	m	
Manuring	m		Manuring	m	
Planting	m	(w)	Planting	m	(w)
Pruning	m		Pruning	m	
Spraying	m		Insecticide	m	
Hulling	m				
Harvesting	m	w	Harvesting	m	w
Transport	m		Transport	m	w
Coffee/Bananas			*Omusiri*[a]		
Weeding	(m)	w	Clearing		w
Cutting grass		w	Planting		w
Mulching	m	w	Weeding		w
Interplanting annuals		w	Harvesting		w
Harvesting annuals	(m)	w			

[a] If a young couple open up *rweya* land for *kibanja*, they normally start with some *omusiri* crops and work together.

types. Curve II A is the input in the *kibanja* and curve III A the input in *omusiri*. These two curves are summed in curve I A to show the total agricultural labour done by women. Curve I B is the labour input by full-time male farmers and curve I C the input of part-time male farmers.

Labour input for animal husbandry has been excluded from the diagram. It should be noted, however, that recording has been done for the farmers keeping cattle. The full-time farmers spent an average of 180 hours per year on herding duties, whereas the part-time farmers mainly employed labourers to do the herding.

Thus it can be concluded that on farm units where people are working full time on farming and where animal husbandry is counted as an integral part of agriculture, *there is no difference in the labour input of men and women,* the average hours worked per year being 1 082 for men and 1 079 for women. These figures, however, only apply to a minority of smallholders.

For the majority of smallholders, 80 per cent or more, the following conclusions can be drawn from Diagram 17. For the *kibanja* land-use section of the farm unit, men do slightly more work than women, but for the whole farm unit consisting of *kibanja* and *omusiri, women do more work than men in terms of input of hours into agricultural field activities.*

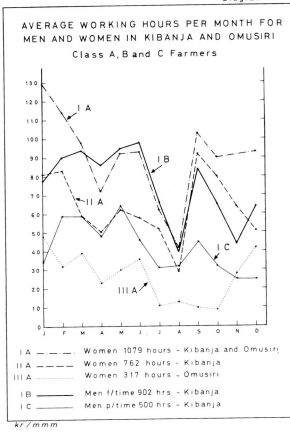

Diagram 17

AVERAGE WORKING HOURS PER MONTH FOR MEN AND WOMEN IN KIBANJA AND OMUSIRI

Class A, B and C Farmers

I A —.—.	Women 1079 hours	Kibanja and Omusiri
II A — — —	Women 762 hours	Kibanja
III A	Women 317 hours	Omusiri
I B ————	Men f/time 902 hrs	Kibanja
I C ————	Men p/time 500 hrs	Kibanja

kr/mmm

months. During the discussion of daylight activity (Diagrams 13 and 14), it was argued that this is not the case where the agricultural work is calculated as the percentage of the total time available during the year. We shall now examine whether this is valid if the agricultural work is estimated on the basis of actual working days available in each month of the survey year.

An absolute minimum number of working days was calculated by deducting the following days from the total days of the year: public holidays = 11, Sundays for Christians and Fridays for Moslems = 52, and market days, meetings, celebrations and days with heavy rain = 52. This gave a total of 250 working days in 1969. For each month the average number of working hours per day was then found by dividing the number of hours in Diagram 17 by the actual number of working days available per month for the three main classes of adults (Table 31).

With a 12-hour day available for daylight activities, there were 3 000 hours available during these 250 days. Of these hours, women spent 36 per cent of the time in agriculture and the full-time men farmers spent 30 per cent.

From August to March women do more work than men, because of the *omusiri* cultivation and the interplanting of the annual crops in the *kibanja*. From March to August men do more work than women, in spite of the fact that they only work in the *kibanja*, owing to the time-consuming nature of banana pruning and ground mulching. The fluctuations between

The Haya evaluation of labour input

When we presented the above conclusions to our Bahaya friends, an interesting reaction took place. The men disagreed and claimed that they were doing more in *agriculture*. Asked to define agriculture, they answered that agriculture is the work applied to bananas and coffee! When then asked what they considered the work done in *omusiri*, the answer was: "That is not really agriculture but some work the women are doing because they like it". This shows the importance of the *kibanja* land-use section in the Haya farming system.

Average daily working hours per month

The use of labour hours in Diagram 17 might give the impression of substantial labour peaks for some of the

Table 31. *Average numbers of hours worked per day in each month of the year (1969). 250 working days*

Months	No. of working days	Women	Men (full-time)	Men (part-time)
January	22	5.9	3.5	1.5
February	19	6.0	4.7	3.1
March	21	4.7	4.7	2.8
April	19	3.8	4.5	2.5
May	20	4.6	4.8	3.2
June	21	4.4	4.7	2.2
July	22	2.8	3.0	1.4
August	21	2.0	1.9	1.5
September	22	4.7	3.8	2.0
October	23	3.9	2.8	1.4
November	19	4.8	2.3	1.3
December	21	4.4	3.0	1.2
Average for	250 days	4.3	3.6	2.0

months according to the division of labour will be understandable from the following description of the agricultural calendar for men and women, respectively.

The agricultural calendar

We have here reproduced the rainfall diagram for the area once again, because the agricultural year can only be understood in relation to the rainy seasons and the dry seasons. (The rainfall was measured by the authors with a 16 cm diameter rain-gauge.)

When examining the agricultural calendar, one quickly notices the relationship between decline in labour activity in agriculture and the main dry season (during the rain peak in April work also declines, but only slightly).

The Haya seasons

The relationship between the climatic seasons and the agricultural year is even more pronounced when one looks at the way the Bahaya divide the year. In Ihangiro the farmers distinguish between four main seasons and within the seasons they have terms for specific periods. (See also Diagrams 1, 2, 3 and 4, pages 12–13.)

Akanda = Mid-December to mid-March.

Etoigo = Mid-March to mid-June (the rain peak has several terms: *oruboza lwa april: boza* = "to decay or to rot"; *kaibisamfula* = "able to make an upright (=honest) person steal."

Ekyanda = Mid-June to mid-September. This is the dry and cool season and the south–east trade wind is dominant. Occasionally, showers can occur in Au-

Weeding the Kibanja.

gust. These are by old people called: *myoyo ya ente* = "souls of cattle."

Omuhanguko = Mid-September to mid-December. *Kuhanguka* = "to begin." The end of this season is called *omusenene,* after the delicious grasshoppers which appear at this time of the year.

Referring to Diagrams 17 and 18, an analysis of the agricultural year will be presented. The main objective is to show how the various agricultural activities with annual and perennial crops are timed in relation to each other and to the division of labour between men and women.

The agricultural calendar in *kibanja* and *omusiri*

Akanda

At the end of December the harvest of the beans planted in September and October starts. The harvest is finished during January and February. When the bean plants stand dry and yellow, the entire plants are pulled out of the ground and are heaped together in front of the house. The beans are threshed from the pods by beating the plants with long sticks. The beans are then dried a few days on the ground, after which they are mixed in a thin paste of clay and water. The paste dries out, providing a hard shell around the bean, thus preserving it better and preventing it from drying during storage. Finally, the beans are stored in large containers made from the leaf sheaths of the banana

Diagram 18

RAINFALL IN mm RWANTEGE, NSHAMBA
1968 – 1970

1968 = 1330 mm   1969 = 888 mm
= monthly rainfall in mm

kr / m m m

Kibanja mulched with banana leaves and stems. In the background the Haya hut.

Omusiri. At the turn of the year the preparation of the groundnut plots reaches its work peak with the planting of the groundnuts mixed with beans. Women who planted bambara nuts in September harvest them during the relatively dry period in February. In March it is time for weeding the groundnuts and beans and some women start to prepare the mounds for sweet potatoes.

Etoigo

This season can be divided into two periods according to the termination of the "Long Rains". The first period during the rains is completely dominated by weeding activity. All the available labour force participates. The soil is loosened with a small stick or weeding knife and the weed is pulled out by hand. The total labour input decreases a bit in April due to the heavy rains.

The second period, commencing in the beginning of May (when the rains abate), is dominated by a single crop—coffee and the activities related to its harvest. This change in agricultural activity is very clearly seen in the two case studies in Diagrams 19 and 20, pages

plant. The containers are hung under the roof in the house. The maize from the *kibanja* is usually harvested continuously as green maize until the end of April.

When the women have finished removing the beans from the *kibanja,* the men can start to prune the bananas, which involves cutting down the outer dried leaf sheaths and dead leaves. Stumps left over after harvest are uprooted and split up and unwanted suckers are dug out. Not only the benefit of proper husbandry but also considerable prestige for the individual farmer is attached to the general appearance of a well-maintained *kibanja.*

If manure is available either in the form of compost or cattle dung, this is the time for manuring. Manure is either mixed into the soil between the stems or spread on the ground around the banana stems.

After finishing these activities the men (together with the women) weed the *kibanja.* It was found that men spent more time weeding at this time of the year in the *kibanja* than women, as the latter are also occupied with weeding the groundnuts in the *omusiri* plots.

Banana plants and coffee trees planted in November are replaced with new specimens, if they have failed to grow.

After the harvest of the maize cobs the stems are pulled out and used as mulch on the ground.

85–86. In Ihangiro *Arabica* coffee is the dominant cash crop; the main harvest is from the beginning of May to the end of June, followed by a final picking in July.

Farmers with *Robusta* coffee can either harvest the unripe cherries in March–April for chewing-coffee or ripe cherries in July–August for sale. During the month of May most of the coffee is picked, and by the month of June the women shift their activities to the *omusiri* plots, as can be seen in Diagram 17. The women have one peak on their labour curve in *kibanja* for the coffee harvest and another small peak on the *omusiri* curve in June for harvesting the groundnuts.

The men and the family members and possibly also hired labour continue with the processing of the coffee berries. After picking, the berries are dried on mats or on the ground (see pictures) in front of the house. When the pulp is dry it is hulled from the bean. This can be done in two ways in Ihangiro.

1. The most common way is to hull the berries on a coffee-hulling rock. The dried berries are spread out on a flat rock and a heavy stone is pulled around among them by means of a rope, whereby pulp and beans are separated (see location of hulling rocks on land-use Map 5). The husk (the separated pulp) and the beans are tossed into the air with the help of a round tray. The wind blows the husk away and the cleaned beans remain on the tray. Finally, the farmer will hand-clean remaining bits of husk from the beans before selling the FAQ (Fair Arabica Quality) coffee to the society.

2. A few farmers in Ihangiro have large wooden machines which resemble mincing machines (their working principle is the same). The berries are hulled by being passed through the machine, after which the husk and the beans are "winnowed" as in method one. This way of hulling is more common north of Ihangiro.

The hulling process is very labour-demanding and hard work. Young farmers do it themselves but all farmers prefer to hire labour for this job if they can afford it. Otherwise they sell the dried unhulled coffee as "Maganda" to the society. The price payed to the farmers for the 1969 coffee was (for FAQ) shs 3/95 and (for *Maganda*) shs 1/55 per kilo. The coffee is tested at the society and the FAQ coffee which does not qualify for the higher grade can either be taken back by the farmer for renewed cleaning or it can be sold as UG (Undergraded). The price of UG in 1969 was shs 1/65 per kilo.

The *eteigo* season is also the time for cutting grass, as the various grass species have grown vigorously during the rains. The grass bundles are piled up in the

The Kibanja is mulched with grass.

kibanja until the coffee harvest is finished, after which they will be spread as mulch, especially in the *kibanja* plots cultivated in the modern way.

Omusiri. During the *etoigo* season the women spend 40 per cent of their time on agricultural activities in their *omusiri* plots. In Ihangiro the dominant *omusiri* crop is groundnuts, possibly mixed with beans, maize, sweet potatoes and cassava. There are two small peaks during this season. After the women have finished the bean harvest in the *kibanja* in February, they start to weed the groundnuts in March; in April and May they harvest the interplanted beans. June is the month for harvesting the groundnuts. The entire plant is dug out of the soil with a hoe and when the nuts have been picked off the stems, the latter are heaped together and burned. Usually women have planted 6–8 small mounds with sweet potatoes in the groundnut plot. The potatoes provide food for the women during harvest time, as the groundnut plots can be several hours' walk from the homestead. The potatoes are fried in the fire made from the groundnut stems.

The groundnuts are brought home during the evening, and dried on the ground in front of the house for a few days; after shelling, most of them are stored in

The family is harvesting coffee Arabica.

large containers made of the leaf sheaths from banana stems. These containers can hold up to 60 kilos of shelled groundnuts; the storage place is again under the roof in the house.

The *omusiri* activities vary considerably from individual to individual. Some women harvest in February and March bambara nuts which were planted in September and October of the previous year. Bambara nuts are the dominant *omusiri* crop in the northern part of Bukoba District. There is virtually an ecological boundary running from Kamachumu to the east. North of this line bambara nuts are the favoured crop; south of this line, groundnuts are dominant. Nevertheless, throughout the District, bambara nuts (*enshoro*) are considered a delicious supplement to the *ebitoke*. Many women spend time hoeing up mounds for sweet potatoes and planting the stems. Sweet-potato cultivation has no fixed period, and may go on throughout the first half of the year. Even as late as August, women plant sweet potatoes in large mounds. The soil in the mounds contain enough moisture for the potato stems to root and survive until the rains start in September, when they can really start growing. (For the moisture-retaining capacity of Bukoba soils, see page 15.)

After the coffee berries are picked, they are spread out on big mats in front of the house to dry in the sun.

Ekyanda

Kibanja. The men continue with the coffee harvest, processing, and selling. Transporting coffee to the society is done mainly on bicycles. One to two sacks of about 60 kilos apiece are carried at a time. The farmers get a first payment upon delivery. When the BCU has sold the coffee through agents in Mombasa in Kenya, a final payment is made to the farmers the following year between April and June. The final payment is calculated on the basis of the price obtained on the world market, after deducting all the appropriate levies.

The grass-cutting on the *rweya* continues and is done mainly by women. A large bundle of grass for mulch weighs about 20 kilos and an adult woman can cut 4–6 bundles a day. About 400 bundles are used for mulching 0.4 ha (one acre). No farmers in our sample with more than 0.5 ha of *kibanja* cultivated in the modern style were able to meet their demand for grass mulch by using only their family labour force. They all either employed additional labourers, paying them either 50

Woman planting the stems of sweet potatoes in the mound.

Woman hoeing up a mound for planting sweet potatoes.

cents per bundle or a bunch of bananas for 4 bundles, or they bought the grass in large quantities from certain collection points.

The mulching of the modern *kibanja* takes place from May to October, with the main work in June, July and August. Some farmers also mulch during the short dry season in February (see Diagrams 18 and 19); the *kibanja* must be completely cleaned of weeds, after which the ground is covered with a thick layer of grass. The purpose of the mulching technique is manifold: to limit the erosion of soil particles by the splashing effects of heavy rain; to add humus to the soil; to reduce the growth of weeds; and to keep the moisture content of the soil at a higher level during the dry season.

Omusiri. A harvest of finger millet or sorghum can take place at the end of June if the bambara-nut plot harvested in February was afterwards planted with millet. Otherwise the very limited activity during the dry season is concerned with the cultivation of sweet potatoes. During August some women plant a crop of maize/beans or sweet potatoes in the black, moist, humus-rich soil in the valley bottoms.

Omuhanguko

Kibanja. At the beginning of this season there is a distinct division of labour between men and women. September is *the* time for pruning bananas and the men continue this work into the next month, but it must be finished before the beans come up.

Women always anxiously await the first showers of the "Short Rains", so that they may start the planting of beans and maize in the *kibanja.* In Ihangiro virtually all *kibanja* was interplanted with beans and maize. The labour curves for both men and women rise this month (Diagram 17) and correlate with the rainfall curve (Diagram 18). 1969 was a "normal" year, but if we look at the rainfall curve for September–October 1968, we can observe that the rain started late that year. After a few showers in August, the rain stopped and many women who planted beans in September had to repeat the planting in October (when the rains really started) —provided they had more beans in stock.

Much of the time from October to December is devoted to the weeding of the beans, that is, in fact, the weeding of the *kibanja,* by both men and women, but the weeding activity declines as the beans gradually form a dense cover over the *kibanja* ground.

If the farmer is expanding his farm unit, the beginning of this season is the time for digging holes for bananas and coffee. During the digging, the topsoil and the sub-soil are kept separate in two heaps. The topsoil is mixed with cattle manure. After some months the topsoil is put back into the hole and the sub-soil is spread on the ground. The coffee trees and the banana plants are planted in November and December; the plants which do not root will then be replaced in March.

Omusiri. In Diagram 17 the curves for the women's work in *kibanja* and *omusiri* approach each other in November and December. This shows how the labour input in *kibanja* declines at the time when the women start on the *omusiri* work of clearing a piece of grassland for cultivation of groundnuts. This work can be combined with the expansion of *kibanja* land or it can be done separately.

Women from the same farm unit often work together, e.g., a mother and a daughter-in-law, but they may work individually on their own elongated groundnut ridges which lie adjacent to each other. *Milala* is the term used for these broad elongated ridges, 4 metres wide and 12–20 metres long.

Two case studies of the agricultural calendar

The two farmers used as examples for distribution of daylight activities for the adult family members are again shown in Diagrams 19 and 20. This time, the total input of the entire labour force for the main activities concerned with the cultivation of perennial and annual crops is shown for each month of the year. The different activities are indicated by the various shadings.

Diagram 19. The total yearly labour input in *kibanja* is 2 235 hours, which is equivalent to 3 192 hours per hectare. Of this total, 78 per cent is the work of the husband, his wife and his mother, the remaining 22 per cent being the contribution of visiting friends and relatives. The husband is 21 years old, the wife 18, and the mother 50.

The various activities of the year are divided into seven main items and the percentage share of the total input for each item is indicated on the graph. (1) *Manuring.* This farmer planted only a few banana plants in 1969. (2) *Hoeing.* Includes digging the holes for bananas. (3) *Grass.* The farmer did not do much mulching, as the *kibanja* consists of traditional *kibanja.* Half of the 3.6 per cent work was cutting grass to put on the floor in the house. (4) *Bananas.* This farmer pruned his bananas slowly during seven months of the year. (5) *Coffee.* Includes picking, drying, processing, transport and selling to the society. The harvest is usually finished in August and the time spent on coffee from September to February is used mainly for processing, transport and selling. That is why we see some hours used on coffee from September to February. He wants to spread his income. (6) *Beans* and maize includes planting in September and October and harvesting during the first months of the year. (7) *Weeding* is the hand-weeding of the entire *kibanja,* and takes place during eight of the twelve months, with a peak in March and April.

The husband's share of the work input in the agricultural calendar is shown in the key to the right in the diagram. It gives an example of the degree of division of labour between the husband and the adult women. He was fully in charge of the husbandry of the bananas, and the key person in the coffee business, since he alone sold the small amount of coffee pro-

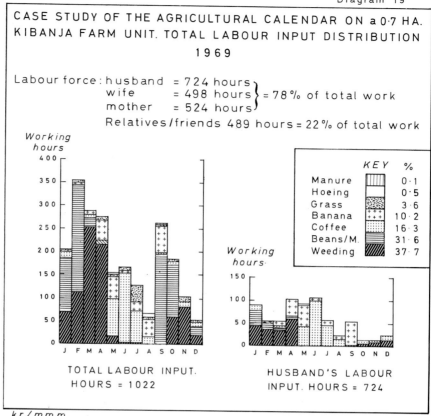

CASE STUDY OF THE AGRICULTURAL CALENDAR ON a 0·7 HA. KIBANJA FARM UNIT. TOTAL LABOUR INPUT DISTRIBUTION 1969

Labour force: husband = 724 hours
wife = 498 hours
mother = 524 hours
} = 78% of total work

Relatives/friends 489 hours = 22% of total work

TOTAL LABOUR INPUT. HOURS = 1022

HUSBAND'S LABOUR INPUT. HOURS = 724

kr/mmm

duced from his *kibanja* that bad year. He gave a hand with the beans and helped with the weeding, but the grass-cutting was left to the women.

Diagram 20. The second case study is from a farm unit of 3.1 ha. The total labour input is 6 940 hours in 1969, that is, 2 339 hours per hectare. The farm unit is about four and half times larger than the farm unit in the first case study and the labour input is about three times larger.

The labour force is composed in the following fashion: *Husband* 55 years old, did 340 hours of work in the *kibanja*. *First wife,* 43 years old, did 812 hours. *Second wife,* 35 years old, did 840 hours. *Third wife,* 28 years old, did 732 hours of work in the *kibanja*. Together these four people did 40 per cent of the work.

Other members of the family, relatives and friends contributed 28 per cent of the total work. Two sons and one daughter aged 15, 9 and 10, respectively, were at school, but permanently living at home. One 18 year-old daughter worked full-time on the farm. Three other daughters and one son, all schoolteachers, contributed

work during their holidays. The rest of this group of workers was made up by visiting relatives and friends. *Employed labour* accounted for 32 per cent of the total labour input and consisted of one permanent hired man and up to 10 casual labourers mainly employed for weeding, coffee processing, pruning bananas, cutting grass and mulching. A certain part of the *kibanja* had been neglected and the weeding had to be done with hoes by employed labourers.

Farmer D is a part-time farmer supervising his labour force. The wives work considerably more in the *kibanja* land-use type than the adult women of farmer C, but the wife and the mother of farmer C put just as many labour hours into the *omusiri* as into the *kibanja,* whereas for the three wives of farmer D, *omusiri* work is minimal. The total number of hours spent on agricultural work by the women from the small unit is more than that of the women from the larger unit, because of the relative importance of *kibanja* and *omusiri* land in the two units.

The main difference between the two farmers is that

Farmer D   Diagram 20

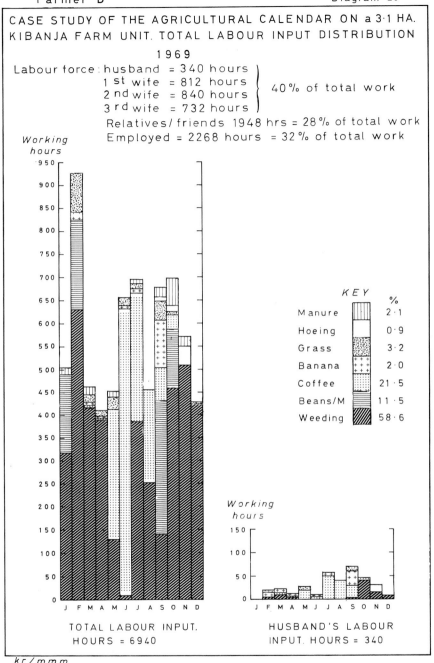

CASE STUDY OF THE AGRICULTURAL CALENDAR ON a 3·1 HA.
KIBANJA FARM UNIT. TOTAL LABOUR INPUT DISTRIBUTION
1969

Labour force: husband = 340 hours
              1st wife = 812 hours
              2nd wife = 840 hours   40% of total work
              3rd wife = 732 hours
              Relatives/friends 1948 hrs = 28% of total work
              Employed = 2268 hours = 32% of total work

KEY   %
Manure   2·1
Hoeing   0·9
Grass   3·2
Banana   2·0
Coffee   21·5
Beans/M   11·5
Weeding   58·6

Working hours

TOTAL LABOUR INPUT.   HUSBAND'S LABOUR
HOURS = 6940   INPUT. HOURS = 340

kr/mmm

the small farmer works more intensively on the food crops, bananas and beans, as he is dependent on a smaller area to produce enough food, even though farmer D has a larger family to support.

Farmer D has 1.8 ha under coffee in monoculture, which is the reason why coffee accounts for a larger percentage of the total input of work. Farmer D's weeding looks impressive; when calculated on a per hectare basis, farmer C used 1 200 working hours per hectare for weeding and farmer D used 1 300 working hours per hectare for the same activity.

The distribution of labour input in *kibanja*

The two previous diagrams showed the proportion of the total labour input devoted to each of the seven main agricultural activities. Although similar trends in priorities were seen, there were certain differences between the two farmers. Table 32 gives the distribution of the seven main items of *kibanja* activities for all the farmers in the labour sample computed on a per hectare basis for the year 1969. One extra activity is added, the planting of trees for fuel, as this was recorded under the *kibanja* activity, although it ought to be separate.

It must be remembered that the year 1969 was a year of low coffee yields in Ihangiro, which accounts for the fairly low figure for the coffee activities. It should also be mentioned that of the 15.3 per cent used for coffee activities, only 0.2 per cent was used for spraying and pruning the coffee trees.

Table 32. *Percentage distribution of the labour input on kibanja activities (1969)*

Activities	Percentage total working hours per ha (1969)
1. Weeding	46.8
2. Beans/maize. Planting and harvesting	16.5
3. Coffee. Harvesting, processing, pruning, spraying, transport and planting	15.3
4. Bananas. Pruning and planting	6.4
5. Grass. Cutting and mulching	7.4
6. Hoeing. Digging holes and clearing land	3.8
7. Manure. Manuring the soil	3.4
8. Planting of trees for fuel	0.4
Total	100.0

Table 33. *Percentage distribution of the labour input on omusiri activities (1969)*

Activities	Percentage total working hours
1. Land preparation	52.4
2. Planting	17.4
3. Harvesting	15.4
4. Weeding	13.5
5. Guarding the crops	1.5
Total	100.0

Hand-weeding, taking up nearly half of the labour time, is obviously an activity to consider. It is debatable whether one can talk about weeding as a bottleneck of the daylight activities. On the other hand, in the present system of individual farming, it is only possible to maintain a large farm unit of *kibanja* if the family labour force is large or if the farmer employs labourers, because of the heavy burden of weeding.

The distribution of labour input in *omusiri*

Table 33 shows the amount of the total labour input used for different activities in the *omusiri* cultivation of various annual crops on the intervillage grassland. Here again one activity—land preparation—accounts for about half of the total labour input.

The hard work of hoeing up the grassland and removing the couch grass is a bottleneck in the present system. As the *omusiri* crops are cultivated on the poorer soils in a system of shifting cultivation, the land preparation must be done every season, and, as population pressure on land increases, the distance to the *omusiri* plots increases.

There is no relationship between size of *kibanja* and the size of *omusiri*. Among the farmers with less than one hectare of *kibanja*, 7 farmers had less than 0.1 ha of *omusiri*, 6 had plots less than 0.2 ha, 5 farmers had plots larger than 0.2 ha and 3 had *omusiri* plots up to 0.7 ha. In fact, the size of the *omusiri* plots varies from year to year according to the health of the adult women on the farm unit, and according to the time available after the *kibanja* has been maintained. The age of the wives and the mothers also means something. It seems that, e.g., mothers and middle-aged women cultivate larger plots than younger women, for whom pregnancy may limit the participation in *omusiri* work.

Total labour input and farm unit size. *Kibanja*

So far we have been concerned mainly with individuals and the allocation of their time between different activities. We shall now consider the relationship between *kibanja* farm size and time spent on agricultural activities, illustrated in Diagrams 21 and 22. Diagram 21 is a scatter diagram of the total input of labour (family, friends and hired labour) on *kibanja* of each farm against the size of *kibanja* on that farm. The scatter is fairly wide among the smaller farmers, as land is not a thoroughly homogeneous variable.

The land variable can and does consist of two main *kibanja* land-use types, which may be more or less labour-intensive (old and modern cultivation techniques). Thus, a *kibanja* unit which is under expansion or just being established needs much more labour input than a well-established one. *Kibanja* units in the former category are those labelled I, II, III, IV and V in the diagrams.

When we test the correlation between labour and land (y and x), we treat labour as the dependent and land as the independent variable. It is possible, however, that land can vary according to labour supply; it is shown below that the correlation is in fact fairly close.

We tested the regression of the total working hours on the *kibanja* size (the regression shows whether there is any significant relationship between labour and land). The regression was first tested for all 31 farmers, then it was tested for the above-mentioned 5 farmers who were actively expanding their *kibanja,* and finally we tested for the remaining 26 farmers who were not expanding. The results of the three tests are shown in the table below; linear equations for the three regression lines are shown in Diagram 21.

Table 34. *Regression of the total working hours on the kibanja size*

Group of farmers	Linear equation	If significant at 99 per cent probability	Corr. coeff.
1) Total 31 farms	$y = 1.83 + 25.60x$	Yes	0.89
2) 5 expanding f.	$y = 12.88 + 32.30x$	Yes	0.99
3) 26 non-exp. f.	$y = 3.36 + 21.02x$	Yes	0.92

The tests show that for all three categories of farmers the relationship is statistically significant. The closest relationship was found for the well-defined small group of expanding farmers. Likewise the 26 non-expanding farmers showed a closer relationship than all the 31 together.

We have previously mentioned that the labour variable conceals heterogeneous components, as the labour input also depends on the composition of the labour force—whether the members are old or young, whether the family is large or small and whether or not hired labour is used. The health condition of the family labour force is also crucial. Therefore, we made another test, as the previous regression used total working hours on *kibanja* work.

In the table below we have correlated total weeding working hours against *kibanja* size. Hand-weeding accounted for nearly half of the total labour input in the *kibanja;* furthermore, weeding is a more well-defined variable, as hand-weeding usually involves a standard rate of work by all types of family labour.

Table 35. *Regression of total weeding hours on the kibanja size*

Groups of farmers	Linear equation	If significant at 99 per cent probability	Corr. coeff.
1) Total 31 farms	$y = 2.7 + 10.59x$	Yes	0.92
2) 5 expanding f.	$y = 10.2 + 8.44x$	No	0.85
3) 26 non-exp. f.	$y = 0.7 + 11.58x$	Yes	0.94

The correlation of weeding hours shows that the 26 non-expanding farmers (maintaining established *kibanja*) have the closest relationship. This relationship is also closer for all 31 farmers than when all agricultural labour activities were considered. It can also be seen that the scatter is not so wide among the smaller farmers in Diagram 22 as in Diagram 21. No significant correlation was found for the expanding 5 farmers, which may be due to the stage of expansion during the survey period. E.g., farmer V was still clearing for expansion, whereas farmers II and IV had started mulching, in which careful hand-weeding is essential. The linear relationship for all 31 farmers is indicated in Diagram 22.

Labour input per hectare per year

Kibanja

The average input of working hours per hectare/year in *kibanja* was 2700 hours, with a range from 1400 to

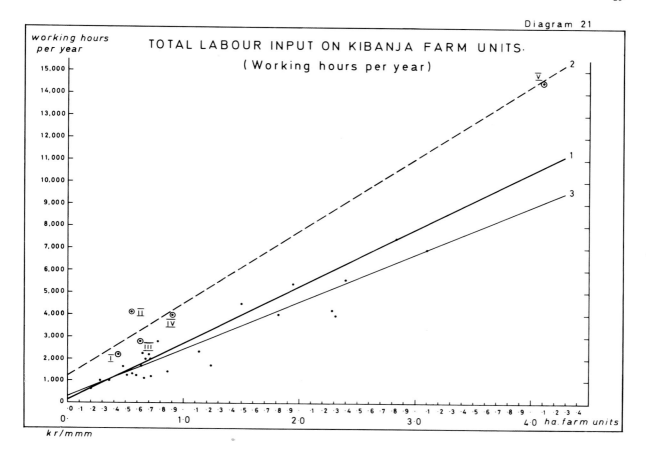

TOTAL LABOUR INPUT ON KIBANJA FARM UNITS.
(Working hours per year)

kr/mmm

5 200 hours for the 31 farmers. For the 26 farmers the average input was 2 500 hours/ha/year, with a range from 1 400 to 3 600 hours. The wide range of hours per hectare reflects the above-mentioned fact that the many components in the two variables, land and labour, can occur in many different combinations, especially for the very small holders. Furthermore, the working hours are made up of many different activities performed by different people.

To take an extreme example, in 1969, a farmer with

Diagram 22

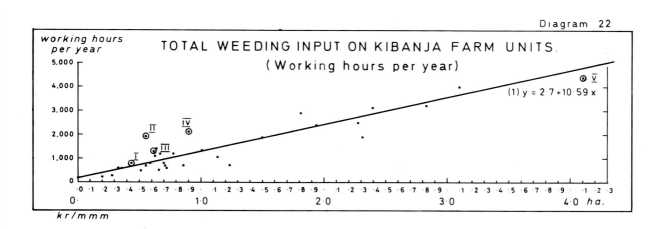

TOTAL WEEDING INPUT ON KIBANJA FARM UNITS.
(Working hours per year)

$(1) \ y = 2 \cdot 7 + 10 \cdot 59 \, x$

kr/mmm

0.55 ha of *kibanja* land used 4 163 hours, of which his sons used about 1 000 hours to walk around collecting manure on the roads, when the cattle were returning to the village in the evening. The farmer was expanding his *kibanja* with only one quarter of a hectare, but he himself had no cows to provide for the manure.

Omusiri

The labour/land ratio in the *omusiri* land-use type fluctuated from 500 to 8 000 hours per hectare per year, depending on the stage of *omusiri* cultivation which the farmer had reached. The low input indicated that the farmer was only harvesting the *omusiri* crop planted the previous year, while a high labour input indicated that the farmer was performing a wide range of *omusiri* cultivation that year.

No relationship was found between *kibanja* unit size and *omusiri* size for the individual farmers. Therefore, only labour input per hectare for the dominant crop mixture groundnuts/beans/cassava was computed, amounting to about 2 200 working hours per hectare per year.

Comparison with A. A. Moody's work[2]

Finally, we shall compare our data with Moody's data from his work in Maruku. Moody undertook a 12-month survey of labour inputs and crop harvests, using recording techniques similar to ours at Ihangiro, among a sample of 23 farmers in Maruku. Maruku is 6 miles south of Bukoba, and the sample was drawn from farmers who sold their tea through the Maruku and Kanyangereko societies. Because his survey also demanded a close degree of farmers' co-operation, he biased his sample in a similar way. Maruku is a much more closely-settled part of Bukoba district, and the population pressure on the land is greater. The average area of *kibanja* among Moody's tea farmers was 0.507 ha, compared with 1.172 ha for the farmers in the Ihangiro time study. Therefore, the personal labour inputs for male and female family members working in *kibanja* were lower in Maruku. During the year, family men in Maruku worked 398 hrs on *kibanja*, while family men in Ihangiro worked 902 hrs. Family women worked 470 hrs in Maruku, and 762 hrs in Ihangiro. Nevertheless, the comparability of our labour data and Moody's Maruku labour data is illustrated by the results of both surveys for total labour annual input, all ages, family, hired and visiting labour, per *kibanja* hectare. The average total in Maruku was 2 933 hrs/ha, and in Ihangiro 2 720 hrs/ha. Friedrich, who suspected that Bahaya farmers were underemployed, or lazy, estimated the total labour input in Kibanja at only 1 341 hrs/ha, less than half the total found in these other, more intensive surveys.

Underestimation of the actual labour inputs of Haya farmers may be one reason for suspecting that they are underemployed or lazy. But further reference to Moody's survey of tea-farmers illustrates that new cash cropping, with better access to loans for further development, can markedly increase the labour input of Haya farmers. In addition to *kibanja* work, male and female family labour in Maruku were working an average of 671 hrs (men), and 280 hrs (women) on the new tea *shambas*. Ihangiro farmers with larger *kibanja* plots worked more hours on *kibanja* than Maruku farmers. Maruku family men, however, worked over 1 000 hrs/year in agriculture, compared with the average 902 hrs/year that Ihangiro farmers worked on *kibanja*.

Finally, it is interesting to note how the introduction of tea into the Haya farming system has affected the traditional division of labour between men and women. In Ihangiro, the men works longer than the women on the *kibanja*, 902 hrs/year, compared to 762 hrs/year. In Maruku, however, the men have become much more involved in the tea-*shambas*, because of the care needed in the maintenance of this important investment. They are always needed in the tea-*shamba* to supervise plucking, and do most of the plucking. They are also almost solely responsible for pruning, mulching and applying fertilizer. Thus, Maruku men now work less time than the women in the *kibanja* plots, but work over twice as much as women in the tea-*shambas*.

Notes

1. Collison's key for man-equivalents (ME)

Age group	10–14	15–19	20–50	over 50
Male (ME)	0.25	0.67	1.00	0.67
Female (ME-	0.25	0.50	0.67	0.50

2. The regressions and the comparative material have been produced with kind assistance from Mr. A. A. Moody. Mr. Moody's fact findings are presented in "A report on farm economic survey of the tea small-holder in Bukoba District". East African Agricultural Economics Society Conference, Dar es Salaam, March 31 to April 4, 1970.

Chapter 7. Production and Gross Return

Measurement of production from the traditionally cultivated *kibanja* caused great difficulties. The yields, especially for coffee, fluctuate from year to year. One year the coffee trees will be heavy with coffee berries, and the next year the same trees will seem empty. In the traditional system, bananas and coffee are interplanted at a wide variety of densities. The authors counted density variations from 700 to 1 500 clumps of bananas per hectare and from 200 to 1 000 coffee trees per hectare in the interplanted cultivation.

The farmers not only interplant coffee and bananas in the *kibanja* but further interplant with benas, maize, pumpkins, sweet potatoes, cassava, tomatoes, pepper, castor-oil plants, orange trees, yams, taros, etc. This system is a highly intensified horticulture system. To show the degree of intensification, the records from one separate plot within a farm unit are listed below. The plot was 0.26 ha in 1969, and the table gives the most important yields from the plot.

Table 36. *Yields from a 0.26 ha kibanja plot*

Crops	kg	No.
Bananas	3 429	
Coffee, fresh	283	
Beans, dried	68	
Sweet potatoes	13	
Pumpkins	185	
Oranges	56	
Cassava	8	
Tomatoes	2	
Bean- and pumpkin-leaves	16	
Maize cobs		291

In Ihangiro beans and maize are interplanted in August and September and harvested from January on. The leaves are picked for spinach in November. When the beans are harvested, pumpkins are interplanted but only in small portions, often near the house. One cannot be certain that the entire *kibanja* area is planted with beans. Some plots in the new-style cultivation or some plots too far away from the homestead can be left out of the annual crop cultivation.

Crops 2 and 3 in the table above are harvested within a limited, short time and can be measured to some accuracy, but all the other crops are harvested from day to day, bananas throughout the year and maize over, e.g., a three-month period. Thus the yield record concentrated on bananas, coffee and beans.

If a farmer has his farm unit divided into, e.g., 6 separate plots in the village, he mixes the coffee harvested from these plots during the processing of the crops. Furthermore, the coffee trees from one plot can be 50 years old and from another plot 2 years old. Even if he normally harvests one plot at a time there can be a second harvest of late-ripening berries from certain plots and not from others. All this caused serious problems in keeping exact records from the separate plots; furthermore, different people in the household harvested the day-to-day crops such as bananas and beans. For that reason we selected 10 plots for special recording; these yields were measured from day to day.

These data were related with records and estimates from experimental plots, Farmers' Training Centres and Agricultural Officers. From the latter informants concordant data was available—and is given below.

Coffee yields

From one hectare of monoculture *Arabica* coffee with 6 year-old coffee trees, the yield should be 675 kg hulled or cleaned coffee (FAQ). That meant (in 1969 prices) a gross return of 2 666/– shs per hectare. The kilo price for cleaned coffee was 3/95 shs (first and second payment included).

If the farmer had chosen to sell his coffee dried (as *Maganda*), his yield would have been 1 227 kg. The kilo price for *maganda* was 1/55 shs, giving him a gross return of 1 902/– shs per hectare (first and second payment included).

For *Robusta* coffee the gross return was 2 315/25 shs for clean coffee per hectare and 2 049/09 shs for *maganda,* the kilo price being 3/43 shs and 1/67 shs, respectively.

Banana yields

One hectare with banana monoculture can yield 750 bunches per year when the plot is well established. The average weight for a bunch was found to be 20 kg. This figure gives a yield of 15 tons of bananas per hectare. At the local market in Ihangiro a bunch of 20 kg could be sold for 3/– shs (in 1969), which would earn the farmer a gross return of 2 250/– shs from one hectare of bananas.

This meant that the farmer could earn 416/– shs more from the *Arabica* cultivation. If the farmer lived in the vicinity of Bukoba town he might be able to sell his bunch at a price of 5/– shs, which would give him a gross return of 3 750/– shs from one hectare, or 1 084/– shs more than from one hectare of *Arabica* coffee. Even with a bunch price of 4/– shs, he would get 334/– shs more from bananas.

This influenced the location pattern of bananas as a cash crop: around Bukoba town many plantations with a banana monoculture could thus be seen coming up in the late sixties. Farmers with easy access to the main road Bukoba–Mwanza also considered shifting to banana cultivation as a supplementary cash crop. Once a banana hectare is established, the labour input demand is low and if the bananas are spaced so widely that a lorry can go between the lines, harvesting the bunches can be made quite effective.

Traditional-cultivation yield

A farmer with mixed coffee and bananas in proportion 1:1 has the possibility of earning a gross return of 2 458/– shs per hectare, 1 333/– shs from coffee and 1 125/– shs from bananas. As the bananas are for consumption, he is left with 1 333/– shs in cash. The average *kibanja* in Ihangiro was 0.7 ha, and our survey revealed that the minimum area which could supply a small family with sufficient food was 0.4 ha of bananas. Thus, 0.3 ha will be available for coffee; from that area a farmer could earn a gross return of about 800/– shs, which should be equal to his yearly income.

Single-plot measurements

How do the above estimated figures relate to the fact-findings in the Ihangiro study? From the single plots with exact measurements, the yields have been computed on a per hectare basis and then converted to gross return in shs.

The gross return from the 10 plots is calculated on the basis of a coffee price of 3/95 shs per kilo for clean

Table 37. *10 single plots. Yields per hectare in kg*

Plot	Clean coffee	Bananas	Comments
1	–	16 000	Monoculture, manured
2	–	17 000	Monoculture, manured
3	125	2 900	Trad.
4	250	400	Trad. very few bananas
5	200	–	Monocul. 3-year-old coffee
6	270	6 570	Trad. *kibanja*
7	150	11 265	Trad. *kibanja*
8	217	13 200	Trad. *kibanja*
9	300	2 535	New style, few bananas
10	222	5 254	Trad. *kibanja*

Arabica coffee and –/15 shs per kilo for bananas (Ihangiro market price, 1969).

The yields in kilos of bananas from plots 1 and 2 compare favourably with the estimated yield of 15 tons per hectare. Both plots are located around the house in the main *kibanja* part, where bananas always show the highest yield due to the refuse from the kitchen and the prestige of having large bananas around one's house. In both cases the plots are heavily manured with either coffee husk or cow manure. Plots 3 and 4 belong to the owner of plot 2 and these two plots with traditional cultivation give considerably lower yields.

The rest of the figures in the table (except plot 5, with young coffee trees) give the yields from a mixed cultivation of coffee and bananas. The yields depend upon the proportional interplanting and the density of the various crops.

Table 38. *Gross return from 10 single plots. Shs per hectare.*

Plot	Coffee	Bananas	Total
1	–	2 400/–	2 400/–
2	–	2 550/–	2 550/–
3	493/75	435/–	928/75
4	987/50	60/–	1 047/50
5	790/–	–	790/–
6	1 066/50	985/50	2 052/–
7	592/50	1 689/75	2 291/25
8	857/15	1 980/–	2 837/15
9	1 185/–	180/25	1 565/25
10	876/90	788/10	1 665/–

Estimated gross return from one ha. clean cof. 2 666/–
Estimated gross return from one ha. banana 2 250/–

(Average yield of beans from the *kibanja* was 335 kg per hectare which is equivalent to 250/– shs in gross return. As the entire *kibanja* area seldom was planted with beans, we have not included this figure in Table 38.)

The gross return in shs in Table 38 is also for comparative reasons given for the estimated gross return from one hectare of monoculture with coffee and bananas.

The plots with monoculture of bananas have already been mentioned as having high yields, whereas plots 4 and 9 (mainly coffee) reflect the bad coffee year 1969, with gross return for coffee under half of the estimated return. Plot 5 (young coffee trees) will come to full bearing 2–4 years later, so the yield is fairly good.

The figures in Table 38 indicate that an expected gross return from one well-maintained hectare of coffee/bananas should be around 2 400/– shs, as the proportion of interplanting will give 2 458/– shs and 2 388/– shs for a coffee/bananas ratio of 1 : 1 and 1 : 2, respectively.

Gross return and income

Friedrich (1968) found in 1964/65 an average gross return of 1 649/– shs from an average holding of 3.5 acres.

91 per cent of the gross return came from 2.0 acres of *kibanja,* which is equivalent to 1 500/– shs return from 0.8 ha. Computed on a per hectare basis, this yields a gross return of 1 875/– shs (in 1964/65 prices). The average gross return from the 10 plots from 1969 is 1 812/– shs.

Friedrich also calculated an hourly rate of family income of –/84 shs, based on the annual earnings being almost equal to the gross return. In our chapter on labour input we obtained an average labour input of 2 700 hours per hectare; with a gross return of 2 400/– shs, this yields an hourly rate of –/89 shs.

Nevertheless, what really counts for the farmer is his actual cash income, which ought to come from the coffee, as the bananas and the annual crops are mainly for consumption. Is he entirely dependent on coffee production or has he other sources of income?

How much money is available for the farmer for expenditure and how does he use this money? These are the questions we shall attempt to answer in the following chapter.

Chapter 8. Household Budgets

(Expenditure pattern)

At the same time as the labour input data were collected among the 31 farmers, we collected data on expenditure and income. We did not, however, aim at a real household budget survey, as we had already experienced many of the problems of the Haya coffee economy. The Haya economy is a mixed food- and cash-crop economy supplemented with income from employment, handicraft and sale of local beer (*pombe*). We concentrated on the distribution of the cash surplus by daily expenditure recording: either the enumerators noted the data on the back of the labour recording sheet or the farmers kept a cash book. (See Appendices 3 and 4.) Although income data were part of the budget survey, we did not press for data at this point, for fear of damaging our good relationships with the farmers. Reliable expenditure data may indicate a minimum amount of cash surplus available to the household. No attempt was made to evaluate the economic return of the home-produced food, nor did we evaluate capital deriving from land, cattle and housing.

Thus, our objective was to throw light on the cash-surplus sector of village life among the farmers in Ihangiro. Given the possibility of obtaining a cash surplus, primarily from a single cash crop (coffee), and from employment, how do people distribute this surplus—what are the trends in their demands?

Expenditure items

The sample was restricted to 25 of the 31 labour-survey households, as 6 households were omitted because of incomplete records.

The household expenditures were divided into 60 different items, which were later amalgamated into 16 main groups.

The last group (16) was kept separately, as it is impossible to get reliable data about peoples' debts and coffee trading. Group 8 is mainly bus transportation. Group 12 (social contributions) are money donations at marriages, baptism or other social events. Group 13 (religious offerings) is money given during services at church. Group 15 is concerned with direct improve-

ments or investments in the farm unit, either the housing facilities or the land or the tilling of the land. Cattle-dip payment was abandoned in August 1969.

Table 39. *60 expenditure items in 16 main groups*

Main groups	Items
1. Food	1. Meat
	2. Fish
	3. Banana (eating)
	4. Banana (*pombe*)
	5. Vegetables
	6. Onions
	7. Spices
	8. Salt
	9. Sugar
	10. Fruit
	11. Bread & cakes
	12. Cassava
	13. Sw. potatoes
	14. Rice
	15. Maize
	16. Maize flour
	17. Other flour
	18. Beans
	19. Groundnuts
	20. Cooking oil
	21. Eggs
	22. Millet, sorghum
	23. Meals outside the house
	24. Other food
2. Drink	25. Local beer
	26. Bottle beer
	27. Milk
	28. Tea (coffee)
	29. Banana juice
3. Cigarettes, etc.	30. Cigarettes, snuff
	31. Sweets
	32. Chewing coffee
4. Personal articles	33. Personal art.
	34. Soap
	35. Paper, books etc.
5. Household equipment	36. Househ. equip.
	37. Furniture
	38. Firewood
	39. Coffee trading
	40. Matches etc.

Main groups	Items
6. Clothes	41. Clothes
7. Bicycle	42. Bicycle
8. Transport	43. Transport
9. Medicine, hospital	44. Medicine, hospital fee
10. School fee	45. School fee
11. Society fee	46. Society fee
12. Social contributions	47. Social contributions
13. Religious offerings	48. Religious offerings
14. Court cases	49. Court cases
15. Investments in house and farmland	50. Housebuilding
	51. Tools
	52. Manure
	53. Grass
	54. Cattledipping
	55. Hired labour
	56. Other expenses
16. Money transactions	57. Repaying debt
	58. Moneylending
	59. Coffee trading
	60. Other

(See also Appendix 5, with a yearly summary of one household.)

Priorities of expenditure items

The ranking of the expenditure items according to the number of households spending money on the various items, regardless of the amount used, gives a first impression of priorities. Table 40 shows the items where all 25 households had expenditure.

Table 40. *Priorities of expenditure items I*

Items	No of households	Range in shs per year	Average shs per year
1. Meat	25	3– 99	48
8. Salt	25	2– 24	9
34. Soap	25	2– 56	19
39. Kerosene	25	2– 36	13
41. Clothes	25	5–249	100

Table 41 continues the ranking of expenditure items according to the numbers of households spending money. Thus, the two tables give the priorities for

about two-thirds of the households. The range in the yearly expenditure per single household is wide, so that the last column gives the average expenditure per year.

Table 41. *Priorities of expenditure items II*

Items	No of households	Range in shs per year	Average shs per year
2. Fish	24	12– 171	56
7. Spices	23	–/10– 13	4
16. Maize flour	23	1– 108	25
36. Househ. equip.	22	3– 263	57
32. Chewing coffee	21	–/20– 25	4
9. Sugar	21	–/40–174	15
27. Milk	20	–/50–165	10
44. Medicine	20	–/80–257	44
6. Onions	19	–/10– 11	2
20. Cooking oil	19	–/20– 40	4
25. Local beer	19	–/30–336	48
47. Social contrib.	19	–/25– 95	22

Table 42, below, gives another order according to the average amount of money spent on the items, thus giving the general trends for peoples' demands when they consider the major posts in their budgets. For priority items 2–6 two-thirds of the farmers used less than 60/– shs per year. Only clothes took on the average a greater share of the budget.

Table 42. *Priorities of expenditure items III*

Priorities	No of households	Average shs per year
1. Clothes	25	100
2. Househ. equip.	22	57[a]
3. Fish	24	56
4. Meat	25	48
5. Local beer	19	48
6. Medicine	20	44

[a] Household equipments=all utensils for the kitchen, sacks, mattresses, beddings, blankets etc.

The scale of expenditure. Income sources

In Chapter 6 we found a correlation between farm unit size and labour input. Using the same sample material for the budget analysis, no correlation was found between farm unit size and expenditure (see Table 43 below). When we compared this with the expenditure pattern from the sample of farmers in Ibwera, we found the same distribution of expenditure among a random sample of farmers. This confirmed the fact that our 25 farmers were representative for a general pattern of expenditure in Bukoba. There seemed to be special components in the Haya economy giving rise to other possibilities of cash earnings.

The 25 farmers were then divided into full-time farmers and part-time farmers; Table 43, below, shows the striking difference in the expenditures of the two groups.

Table 43. *Expenditure of full-time and part-time farmers*

Full-time farmers			Part-time farmers		
Farmer	Exp. per year (shs)	kibanja (ha)	Farmer	Exp. per year (shs)	kibanja (ha)
3	183	0.33	1	506	0.20
6	342	0.51	2	506	0.28
8	620	0.56	4	1 737	0.36
10	158	0.64	5	1 012	0.43
12	97	0.67	7	1 272	0.55
15	275	0.72	9	1 070	0.59
16	579	0.78	11	1 238	0.66
18	1 130	0.90	13	1 253	0.70
19	834	1.13	14	856	0.71
22	614	1.81	17	1 162	0.86
24	516	2.40	20	1 046	1.23
25	658	2.83	21	1 340	1.50
			23	1 267	2.31

Only one of the full-time farmers had expenditures exceeding 1 000/– shs, and only three of the part-time farmers were below 1 000/– shs per year in expenditures.

Income sources

The Haya peasant agriculture is based on a division of labour between men and women, men being in charge of the perennial crops, bananas and coffee, and the women taking care of the annual crops. It is characteristic for this agricultural system, which cultivates the perennial crops in the traditional way, that they, once established, are less labour-demanding than the annual crops, thus leaving the opportunity for increasing income through non-agricultural work by the men. This is underlined in Diagrams 13 and 14 in Chapter 6, indicating that even a full-time male farmer will have more leisure time than a full-time female farmer. This gives him the opportunity to take up casual work if he wishes.

The part-time farmer uses double the amount of time on non-agricultural work as on agriculture. Either he keeps his *kibanja* unit to such a size that it can be maintained by family members or he employs labourers as a substitution for his own labour input. This is profitable as long as a cheap labour force is available, e.g., from Burundi or Rwanda.

The Haya economy can to a certain degree be described as a dual economy with a subsistence sector and a money sector. The subsistence factor produces food for consumption and is the basis of rural life. The subsistence output is defined as: "output arising from outside the recorded market economy" (Livingstone and Ord 1969). Very few families in Bukoba live entirely at a subsistence level; nearly all participate in the money economy. The dual economy is so young that whether you are a craftsman, a clerk, a teacher of a Principal Secretary in Dar Es Salaam, you maintain your *kibanja* unit at home as part of your private economy. The specialization and division of labour arising from a dual economy is still at an initial stage and gives rise more to increased consumption or small-scale investments in agriculture than to a complex exchange economy.

Nevertheless, the dual economy creates a range of income possibilities and makes the analysis of the income sector and thereby the whole agricultural system more complex. A detailed investigation of the income sector and its sources reveals that it is too simple to talk about a food- and a cash-crop sector only. An analysis of the part-time farmers in the sample makes it evident that the part-time farmers often obtain a higher income from non-agricultural work. Table 44 gives an outline of the diversified economy of the part-time farmers.

One should also remember that 1969 was a bad coffee year in the survey area and selling bananas could be an adjustment to this situation, e.g., farmers 4, 21 and 23. We are not sure this is the case. Farmer 4 had uprooted all his coffee trees to get sufficient food from his 0.36 ha plot, relying on cash from his salary as a clerk. Farmer 21 was buying bananas from farmers in the villages and selling them to private traders coming around to certain collecting points weekly. These traders had organized the export to the Mwanza and the Dar Es Salaam markets. Farmer 23 had a large share of his *kibanja* as a pure stand of bananas and had for several years produced bananas as part of his cash crops.

On the other hand, bananas were in the late sixties coming up as a supplementary cash crop recommended

Table 44. *Income sources for part-time farmers 1969 (shs)*

Farmers	Gross income (shs)	Part of total income deriving from				
		coffee	bananas	*pombe*	salary wage loan	Occupation
1	483	12	12	–	345	Casual lab.
2	1 441	611	91	388		Brewer
4	3 080	–	143	–	845[b] 1 645	Clerk
5	2 129	803	8	52	1 234	Sawyer
7	1 439	213	83	114	646	Mason
9	1 369	67	20	54	770[b] 155	Casual lab.
11	2 303	890[a] 145	28	–	917	Hairdresser
13	1 259	435	20	–	300	Casual lab.
14	672	117	13	–	400	Carpenter
17	1 291	519	19	509	–	
20	1 402	100	14	–	1 260	Evangelist
21	1 394	1 050	252	64	–	Trader
23	2 303	396	450	479	905	Manager[c]

[a] Second payment for coffee from previous year received in 1969.
[b] Loan obtained either from the Cooperative Society, the Church or private.
[c] Piecework contract with nearby coffee estate for providing of grassmulch. Employs Rwanda labourers for this work.

by the BCU. In 1970 the BCU started the establishment of special Primary Society Banana plots. The constantly falling coffee prices in the sixties were also an incentive to diversify agricultural production. Nevertheless, it was primarily the farmers near the Bukoba town market who benefited from banana cultivation as a cash crop.

Income from coffee

In 1969 a farmer with a high-yield one-hectare monoculture coffee *Arabica* could earn a gross income of about 2 600 shs on clean coffee. If he sold his coffee dried, his gross income would be 1 900 shs. That is to say, the coffee income figures in Table 44 must be read with care. None of the *kibanja* hectares in Table 44 are pure stands of coffee. Farmer 2 had no chance of getting 611 shs from 0.28 ha (concerning hectares see Table 43). This means that the 611 shs do not derive from his own coffee alone, but also from trading with coffee.

It should also be emphasized that the column with gross income in most cases compares fairly well with the expenditure figures in Table 43. On the income side the survey could not trace the flow of money from, e.g., salary or wage income going into trade or the moneylending business, which accounts for our inability to give the full picture of all the income sources.

Pombe sale

The brewing and selling of local beer (*pombe*) or distilled beer (*konyagi*) can only earn the producer a small net income. Normally the brewer will not be self-sufficient in beer, bananas and sorghum and he must invest in these items. For example, 2 bought bananas and sorghum for 185/– shs and farmer 17 bought for 344/– shs. It must also be borne in mind that a considerable amount of work must be invested in production. Friedrich (1968) mentioned 25 working hours needed to produce 220 lbs of beer. At least three times as much time is needed for *konyagi* production.

Salary and wage income

The definition of a part-time farmer is also questionable within the context of the present Haya economy. Is farmer 4 a clerk with a supplementary agricultural activity; is the evangelist first a clergyman and then a farmer? We choose to keep the term part-time farmer, as both the clerk and the evangelist will, in case of unemployment, rely on the farm unit for their living. Thus, the basis in the village life is the land and agricultural production. The non-agricultural work can, if stable, bring higher income than agriculture. Furthermore, the person with extra cash income can

Table 45. *Income sources for full-time farmers 1969 (shs)*

| Farmer | Gross income | Part of total income deriving from | | | |
		coffee	bananas	*pombe*	casual work
3	459	78	87	20	–
6	119	5	–	–	101
8	653	133	3	–	208
10	40	–	5	30	–
12	26	–	8	3	–
15	420	196	11	–	–
16	329	237	–	20	–
18	1 155	209	176	–	280
19	970	271	250	123	–
22	351	190	5	157	–
24	800	604	8	179	–
25	1 020	628	22	47	–

Table 47. *Fluctuation in coffee gross income 1968 and 1969. Mainly Robusta. Random sample Kanyigo*

Kibanja ha	Gross income 1968 shs	Gross income 1969 shs
0.9	177	1 541
1.2	257	1 141
0.7	286	459
0.4	931	1 722
0.5	304	170
1.0	732	724
0.6	274	488
0.5	410	715
0.9	441	1 336
0.3	236	1 414
1.8	1 577	1 975
0.6	344	570
0.2	199	392

take advantage of the capitalistic structure of the Haya society and exploit the possibilities for trading and moneylending.

Income scale for full-time farmers

The income from coffee was unusually low in 1969; e.g., farmer 24 received 1 800/– shs in 1968, when the coffee price dropped to the lowest level in many years. The fluctuation is mainly due to the age of the coffee trees and to husbandry. Many coffee trees are 50 years old or more and few farmers prune their old coffee trees. Only 17 per cent of the total *kibanja* area was planted and cultivated in the modern way, which gives a smaller fluctuation in yields, and many modern plots were in 1969 quite new.

Table 46. *Fluctuation in coffee gross income 1968 and 1969. Mainly Arabica coffee. Random sample Ibwera*

Kibanja ha	Gross income 1968 shs	Gross income 1969 shs
0.8	870	88
1.1	718	201
1.3	435	18
0.9	650	212
0.8	223	47
0.9	291	194
0.7	140	12
0.6	136	27
0.8	361	56
1.1	732	225

Tables 44 and 45, incomplete as they are, show that coffee is not a substantial income source for the smallholder; only by supplementing his income from non-agricultural work can he maintain a decent standard of living. The problem of fluctuation is severe and general, as may be seen in the following tables from other areas in the District.

The fluctuation varies from area to area, depending on whether the dominant crop is *Arabica* or *Robusta*. During a random sample with a single interview it is impossible to check for fluctuations caused by coffee trading. Therefore, we finally checked with some rich farmers whom we knew were only selling coffee produced from their own farm unit.

The *kibanja* hectares are listed to show how different the yield can be from the same number of hectares.

The fluctuations vary from a few hundred shillings to several thousand from one year to the next. The price of *Robusta* coffee was nearly the same (only a few cents higher in 1969). *Arabica* coffee FAQ went up with 50 cents per pound from 1968 to 1969. No attention is here paid to other factors which could influence the yield, such as coffee berry diseases, caterpillar attacks, climate, etc. We merely wish to point out this special condition of the Haya economy.

It is obvious that this insecure flow of income can have disastrous effects on the family life of the Bahayas. If, e.g., a family is struck by illness in a bad coffee year and must spend a considerable amount on hospital treatment, it may be necessary to borrow or mortgage on the expected good yield the following year. Thus the fluctuation of coffee yields can easily drive the smallholder, with no savings, into a vicious circle of moneylending. We shall in the last chapter see how the moneylender takes this into account when he operates.

Table 48. *Fluctuation in coffee gross income. Rich farmers. Ibwera and Kanyigo 1968 and 1969 (shs)*

	Ibwera			Kanyigo	
Kibanja ha	1968	1969	Kibanja ha	1968	1969
			2.1	1 184	4 688
2.4	2 601	1 809	0.9	126	816
5.2	2 212	641	1.8	670	3 359
2.1	5 317	1 532	1.7	2 459	3 129
2.0	1 923	811	2.2	2 370	3 620
2.1	1 504	812	1.3	884	2 362

The patterns of expenditure

Will the different levels in income influence the expenditure patterns for part-time and full-time farmers? The following tables show the expenditure divided into the amalgamated groups for both types of farmers.

If Tables 49 and 50 are compared with Table 42, the priorities of expenditure patterns can be recognized. As all food items are summed up in group 1, it is evident that all farmers supplement their own food

production by buying. The main items of food purchases are meat and fish, as can be seen in Tables 51 and 52.

There is no marked difference in meat and fish consumption by part-time and full-time farmers. On an average, farmers spend a little more on fish, which is dried and smoked fish from Lake Victoria. Both part-time and full-time farmers spend relatively more money on extra food supply than on other items per year.

Drink

There is no indication in Tables 49 and 50 that Haya men are heavy drinkers or that they waste a good deal of money on beer. A few spent a fair amount on beer (e.g., 7, 9 and 18) but the rest have what one might call a normal behaviour, enjoying life from time to time. How much beer people produce from their own bananas cannot be seen here, but the social role of beer in the Haya society should be remembered.

Farmer 20 is an interesting exception from the general pattern, using 165/- shs on milk. The wife in that family was the local leader of the Bethania society. She gave many courses about family health and diet to the women. Her own budget was an example of a properly composed diet.

Otherwise, all the smaller amounts under the item "drink" are mainly used for beer, although a small share is spent for buying tea. Among the well-to-do

Table 49. *Part-time farmers' expenditure in 1969 (shs)*

Groups	1	2	4	5	7	9	11	13	14	17	20	21	23
1. Food	258	413	194	692	223	263	668	237	228	574	551	214	237
2. Drink	13	66	17	13	358[b]	236[b]	39	64	3	73	206[c]	69	49
3. Cig., etc.	10	/40[a]	2	10	121	24	152	19	8	2	–	9	36
4. Personal art	34	13	51	12	35	53	21	29	42	19	63	26	2
5. Househ. equip.	46	17	346	116	58	267	91	75	49	32	58	144	107
6. Clothes	59	105	243	89	127	87	64	196	99	107	83	151	218
7. Bicycle	5	30	31	17	19	–	19	277	49	145	13	24	–
8. Transportation	18	–	10	–	17	20	11	14	9	21	–	37	127
9. Med. hosp.	11	35	257	–	36	71	65	138	56	4	4	60	223
10. School fee	–	–	–	62	40	–	–	20	25	78	60	20	175
11. Society fee	15	–	70	–	58	–	–	–	56	50	–	–	–
12. Social cont.	32	23	95	–	17	42	23	54	79	10	–	29	7
13. Rel. off.	/20	–	3	/40	12	/10	/30	/35	25	20	--	1	7
14. Court case	–	–	–	–	–	–	–	50	–	–	–	–	25
15. Investment in house/farm	5	6	418	2	152	–	85	81	129	29	7	557	55

[a] /40 means 40 cents: otherwise all figures are rounded up to nearest whole number.

[b] Local beer 336 shs and 235 shs.

[c] Milk 165/10 shs and tea or instant coffee 41/25 shs.

The butcher's shop in Nshamba village in Ihangiro.

farmers it has become modern to drink instant coffee from the factory in Bukoba town, but this is still so expensive that it is reserved for the few.

Cigarettes

Smoking habits have a similar regular pattern. A few smoke a lot but the majority have a very modest consumption. Many farmers grow their own tobacco and smoke pipes.

Household equipment and clothes

There is a marked difference between the part-time farmers and the full-time farmers concerning the purchase of household equipment and clothes. This could be due to the bad coffee harvest, as the two items are one and two on the priority list. All farmers (except one) with an expenditure of more than 1 000/- shs per year spent between 100/- shs and 250/- shs on clothes. Farmers with less than 1 000/- shs expenditure per year spent less than 100/- shs on clothes. If a family had children at school, school uniforms have been listed under this item.

Items 7–15

Part-time farmers spent more on *bicycles* and *transport action*, which might be necessary for their non-agricultural work. The bicycle expenditure was minor repairs and spare parts. The transportation was primarily bus tickets.

Medicine and *hospital fees* accounted for larger amounts among part-time farmers, as this group can afford to utilize the mission hospitals, where they must pay for treatment and medicine, whereas the full-time farmers with lower income will use the Government hospitals or clinics, where treatment and medicine are free of charge. This is not because the part-time farmers preferred to pay, but because the Government clinics often ran out of medicine. The economic burden of hospital treatment can be seen in farmers 4 and 23.

Table 50. *Full-time farmers' expenditure in 1969 (shs)*

Groups	3	6	8	10	12	15	16	18	19	22	24	25
1. Food	153	135	196	126	14	31	386	406	119	223	388	189
2. Drink	8	5	23	4	–	13	5	163[a]	85[a]	6	25	52
3. Cig., etc.	–	1	17	1	/20	14	5	78	143	10	16	9
4. Personal art	4	23	30	1	12	5	8	59	2	17	5	28
5. Househ. equip.	4	13	39	7	12	21	53	102	272	13	2	23
6. Clothes	8	53	94	5	44	62	107	249	98	10	21	112
7. Bicycle	–	9	/35	–	–	–	–	–	–	–	40	23
8. Transportation	3	3	36	–	–	23	–	–	–	28	4	1
9. Med. hosp.	2	29	17	–	–	/80	–	5	70	–	6	23
10. School fee	–	–	–	–	–	–	–	–	10	200	–	35
11. Society fee	–	50	50	–	–	50	–	–	–	102	–	–
12. Social cont	3	2	55	–	–	–	–	34	3	/25	3	47
13. Rel. off.	–	–	1	–	–	/80	–	–	–	/20	2	1
14. Court case	–	–	–	–	–	–	–	–	–	–	–	–
15. Investment in house/farm	–	12	62	15	16	55	15	34	33	4	6	115

[a] Local beer 161/- shs and 83/- shs.

Shop with clothes. Nshamba village in Ihangiro.

Society fees (membership fees for the Bukoba Cooperative Union) are normally paid between June and August, when farmers get their first payment for the coffee. In a bad coffee year some farmers postpone the payment to the following year. In some cases, it seems, the farmers may have forgotten to list this expenditure, as it can have been deducted from their coffee payment.

The social contributions and the *religious offerings* differ greatly in size. This is not only due to the fact

Table 51. *Meat and fish expenditure 1969. Part-time farmers (shs)*

	1	2	4	5	7	9	11	13	14	17	20	21	23
Meat	22	61	50	62	42	23	95	34	4	77	143	57	79
Fish	33	109	15	121	52	45	113	70	33	113	46	50	35
Total	55	170	65	183	94	68	208	104	37	190	189	107	114

Table 52. *Meat and fish expenditure 1969. Full-time farmers (shs)*

	3	6	8	10	12	15	16	18	19	22	24	25
Meat	57	4	47	45	3	7	68	99	51	15	32	26
Fish	56	13	22	7	–	12	171	34	29	58	69	89
Total	113	17	69	52	3	19	239	133	80	73	101	115

Shopkeeper in Nshamba. In front tins with kerosene.

Marketday in Orumunasi, an Ujamaa Village in Ihangiro.

that many farmers pay in kind to the church: in the social sector there is a constant flow of small amounts of 1/– to 2/– shs among people. There are numerous events in social life when people visit a relative or a friend and contribute some small amount to the head of the household. In the social sector your contribution is a very personal thing, whereas in the church it is more anonymous. Therefore the five-cent pieces in the basket on Sundays in the churches are numerous.

Investments in housing or in the farm unit, i.e., the land and cultivation, are primarily made in the latter item. Among part-time farmers expenditure for hired labour, grass for mulching and manure (Farm Yard Manure) are common. The expenditures in this sample on housing consist of minor repairs or renewals, such as a door or a window, as no farmer built a new house during the survey. For comparison we give the expenditures for building a simple house with clay walls and a corrugated roof.

Table 53. *Expenditure for building one house. 1969 (shs)*

1. Poles and other wooden material	95/15
2. Nails	14/–
3. Digging holes for poles	1/40
4. Iron sheets	360/–
5. Sheet covers	45/–
6. Sheet nails	21/–
7. The builder's salary	80/–
8. The soil mixer's salary	95/–
9. Debbes and elephant grass	10/–
10. Six doors	240/–
11. The collector of poles	19/50
12. Four windows	40/–
13. Food for all the builders	20/–
Total expenditures	1 041/05

General trends in the expenditure pattern

We can now sum up the general trends in the Ihangiro expenditure pattern, as revealed by Tables 49 and 50. Diagram 23 shows the share each amalgamated group takes of the total expenditure budget for all farmers (in percentages). Food is dominant, with nearly 35 per cent of the total, next comes clothes, with about 12 per cent and third, household equipment, with 9.6 per cent. Investments in housing and farm unit account for 9.3

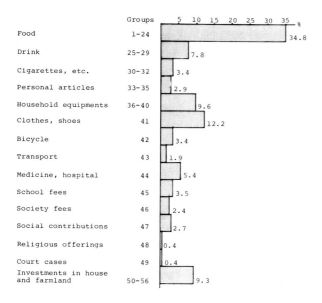

Diagram 23. Expenditure groups in percentage of
total expenditure budget

	Groups	%
Food	1-24	34.8
Drink	25-29	7.8
Cigarettes, etc.	30-32	3.4
Personal articles	33-35	2.9
Household equipments	36-40	9.6
Clothes, shoes	41	12.2
Bicycle	42	3.4
Transport	43	1.9
Medicine, hospital	44	5.4
School fees	45	3.5
Society fees	46	2.4
Social contributions	47	2.7
Religious offerings	48	0.4
Court cases	49	0.4
Investments in house and farmland	50-56	9.3

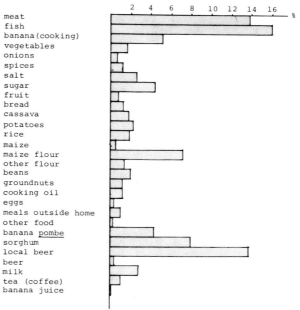

Diagram 24. Percentage of 29 food and drink items of the
food and drink sector

per cent and then expenditure used on mainly local
beer comes in with 7.8 per cent. Lastly, money spent
on medicine and hospital can be mentioned, accounting
for 5.4 per cent of the total budget.

These percentages are average figures intended to
show trends. From Tables 49 and 50 it is seen that the
dispersion is wide. If the group "food" is broken down
and rearranged, it is found that 8 of the 25 farmers used
between 10–20 per cent of their total expenditure on
food. Six farmers used between 20–40 per cent and a
similar number used between 40–60 per cent. Three
farmers used 60–80 per cent of their expenditure on
food and only two used more than 80 per cent, namely
83 per cent each, but that was of a yearly expenditure
budget of 158/– shs and 183/– shs, respectively. Among
the full-time farmers there was a tendency towards
using a greater share of money for food expenditure
with decreasing amount available. This is illustrated in
Table 54.

The same tendency cannot be seen among part-time
farmers with an expenditure budget of more than
1 000/– shs. Thus, farmer A, with 1 070/– shs of total
expenditure, used 26 per cent for food, whereas
another farmer B, with 1 012/– shs expenditure, used 69
per cent for food. The latter had a smaller family but he
had a fairly new *kibanja,* while farmer A had a family of
5 but an old well-producing *kibanja.* Thus, many
factors can produce quite different results in the
amounts used for food within similar-sized budgets.

Food and drink sector

Food and drink account for 42.5 per cent of the total
expenditure budget for all farmers. The importance of
meat and fish has already been mentioned, and in
Diagram 24 the food and drink sector has been split
into 29 base items.

The proteins—meat, fish, beans, groundnuts, eggs
and milk—account for 36 per cent of the food and drink
sector. Beans and groundnuts are grown by the Ihangiro people. The beans are harvested in January and
February and the groundnuts in June and July, so that
the farmers have a vegetable protein supplement to
their starchy food.

Table 54. *Full-time farmers 1969*

Percentage total expenditure used for food	amount in shs
14	834
29	658
33	620
36	614
46	579
45	516
83	183
83	158

Maize flour is popular and about 7 per cent is spent on this item. The interplanted maize in the *kibanja* is mainly consumed as roasted cobs. Milk is bought in small quantities. Some of the farmers lived near a Farmers' Training Centre, where milk was available for sale. Only 20 per cent of the farmers reared cattle, and then primarily for manure, so that milk was generally in short supply.

From Diagram 24, one might gain the impression that the people in Ihangiro are fairly well off concerning proteins, as compared with other regions in Tanzania. This is true, but if we look at how often people buy these items, the situation is not so impressive.

Number of purchases per year

People in Ihangiro could buy one pound of meat (with bone) for one shilling in 1969. They paid 1/50– shs for one pound of pure meat and 2/– shs for fillet. This means that the sample family which spent most on meat, 143/– shs, bought 96 pounds of meat in one year (using the the 1/50 price). The farmer spending least bought 2 pounds of meat during the year.

Another way of illustrating the amount of the different food items people bought in one year's time is to look at the number of purchases in 1969. Meat and fish and perishable items were bought the same day they were to be consumed. Other items like sorghum, rice and maize flour, were sometimes bought in larger quantities. Nevertheless, a general habit in a small-scale economy is to buy in small quantities.

The number of purchases per year is illustrated in Tables 55 and 56, below. In the present tables, we are only concerned with protein items which people did not produce from their own farm unit, as well as a few other items such as spices, salt, sugar, tea and rice. Finally, we should also note such items as beer and cigarettes.

If the number of purchases are summed, the full-time farmers will buy these items at most every sixth day and half of the families every eighth day or at even longer intervals. Half of the part-time farmers bought meat and fish every sixth day or more often.

Eggs are bought very seldom and the value of eggs was not recognized; certain taboos also existed.

Milk is normally bought when there is a newborn child in the family, unless the family can borrow a cow for a certain time or obtain the milk as a gift from a cow-owner. Within the social structure of the Haya society there is a distribution of milk based on friendship and family relations. Tinned milk which can be bought in the small shops in the villages is hardly purchased. Again, it is obvious that farmers with supplementary income from non-agricultural work buy more milk, even if the quantities are very small. The striking feature in the mixed Haya husbandry is that there is so little milk for distribution. Milk is still a rare commodity in the Haya family life. (See notes to Chapter 4.)

Spices consist mainly of curry powder, which is used for the *ebitoke* (the banana meal), but not as an everyday article. Spices are bought when people want to make a special delicious meal when guests have arrived, etc.

Salt is a necessary commodity bought by all farmers, whereas sugar is used primarily for tea; it may thus be seen that heavy tea-drinkers buy more sugar than others.

Rice in the Haya diet is a luxury for feasts such as

Table 55. *Number of purchases for part-time farmers 1969*

Items	1	2	4	5	7	9	11	13	14	17	20	21	23
Meat	15	21	20	21	23	8	38	19	2	29	89	29	21
Fish	38	70	9	50	43	40	87	60	22	63	24	26	15
Eggs	–	–	–	–	–	–	1	2	–	–	12	6	–
Milk	10	2	7	1	4	2	9	4	1	2	66	5	–
Spices	29	19	–	15	10	25	67	43	16	7	16	2	–
Salt	43	34	5	5	56	17	21	26	30	31	21	31	7
Sugar	6	2	13	7	5	7	40	11	10	1	82	27	–
Tea	4	1	4	1	24	1	6	3	4	1	40	15	–
Rice	3	1	1	13	–	5	11	2	1	1	2	1	1
Local beer	1	39	–	2	261	64	15	57	–	39	–	19	15
Cigarettes	5	–	–	20	292	60	282	7	–	–	–	19	14

Table 56. *Number of purchases for full-time farmers 1969*

Items	3	6	8	10ᵃ	12ᵃ	15ᵃ	16	18	19ᵇ	22ᵃ	24	25ᵃ
Meat	31	2	30	20	2	4	22	33	34	6	13	11
Fish	37	17	17	3	–	10	60	17	27	28	29	39
Eggs	–	–	3	–	–	–	–	1	–	1	–	–
Milk	4	1	3	2	–	–	–	1	2	–	1	2
Spices	25	15	39	17	–	2	9	8	11	6	17	9
Salt	35	19	18	8	7	27	6	6	26	39	2	47
Sugar	–	–	41	6	–	1	2	11	1	4	3	19
Tea	–	–	16	1	–	–	–	2	–	–	2	9
Rice	–	1	6	–	–	–	2	2	–	–	1	1
Local beer	–	3	4	1	–	8	2	24	25	4	–	25
Cigarettes	–	–	–	–	–	40	7	71	324	14	48	19

ᵃ Cattleowners.
ᵇ Poultry owner.

Christmas meals or meals at wedding celebrations. Many farmers buy rice only once or twice a year, either when they get their first payment for the coffee or in December for Christmas.

Beer and cigarettes sometimes go together (e.g., farmer 7) and can take quite a part of the expenditure budget. Farmer 7 spent 336/– shs on beer and 94/– shs on cigarettes in 1969. Farmer 11 spent 130/– shs on cigarettes and farmer 19 also spent 143/– shs on cigarettes. Sometimes this expenditure meant that the family had to do without necessities. E.g., farmer 7 spent 430/– shs on beer and cigarettes but only 94/– shs on meat and fish. Farmer 19 used 225/– shs on beer and cigarettes and 79/– on meat and fish.

Generally the luxury sector, the last two items, is modestly used, as people buy in very small quantities, e.g., two cigarettes per time—such as farmer 15, who bought cigarettes 40 times that year but only spent 13/– shs.

These tables, like Tables 49 and 50, illustrate that some farmers are fairly well off and some have nearly a subsistence living. In this sample there is no example of a truly rich farmer with a large productive farm unit and supplementary employment. Nevertheless, the material clearly indicates the advantage of having access to income outside the agricultural section. This feature is part of the development which has come in with the money economy introduced by the Europeans. This development has been unequally distributed and has created classes in rural society.

To illustrate this economic class difference, four families will be analysed in detail. Two are living near a subsistence level, one is an average full-time farmer type, and the last represents the well-off part-time farmer.

Case studies of household budgets

The subsistence budget

The first family consists of a woman, 39, living together with her mother, 62, and two daughters, 11 and 9. She has a *kibanja* of 0.67 ha, of which 0.57 ha is cultivated in the traditional style with coffee and bananas mixed, and 0.1 ha is planted in the modern way with coffee and a few rows of bananas. On the nearby *rweya* she cultivated 0.12 ha with groundnuts, beans, a little maize, sweet potatoes and cassava. Adjacent to this plot she had planted last year's groundnut plot with finger millet. The family and various visitors used 2 060 hours of labour input in the *kibanja* and 1 716 hours in the *omusiri*. She had two cows.

Her total yearly expenditure was 97/15 shs, of which 60/– shs were spent in August. Going through the monthly expenditure, a very modest standard of living is illustrated. Farmer 12:

	Purchases	shs	Monthly total
January	Onions	–/10	
	Spices	–/10	
	Salt	–/20	
	Soap	–/90	
	Kerosene	–/60	
	Cattledip	–/80	2/70
February	Chewing coffee	–/20	
	Kerosene	–/20	
	Cattledip	–/60	1/–

	Purchases	shs	Monthly total
March	Salt	–/30	
	Kerosene	–/50	
	Cattledip	–/60	1/40
April	Sorghum	9/–	
	Soap	1/30	
	Kerosene	–/20	
	Matches	–/35	
	Cattledip	–/80	11/65
May	Meat	1/50	
	Soap	2/10	
	Kerosene	–/30	
	Firewood	4/50	
	Cattledip	–/80	9/20
June	Salt	–/20	
	Househ. equip.	–/40	
	Cattledip	–/60	1/20
July	Salt	–/20	
	Soap	1/–	
	Kerosene	–/40	
	Cattledip	–/60	2/20
August	Personal art.	–/50	
	Soap	–/50	
	Househ. equip.	2/50	
	Kerosene	1/80	
	Clothes	40/–	
	Cattledip	10/70[a]	60/–
September	Salt	–/20	
	Soap	1/50	1/70
October	Salt	–/10	
	Soap	1/80	1/90
November	Soap	–/40	–/40
December	Meat	1/50	
	Salt	–/20	
	Soap	1/60	
	Kerosene	–/40	
	Matches	–/10	3/80

[a] In August the dipping was done free of charge and people paid their debts.

We have made this example so detailed because it illustrates better than many words the life of this family. Salt, soap and kerosene are the necessities. In August she spent two-thirds of her yearly expenditure as she could afford to buy two pieces of clothes of 22/– shs each. That was the time where she sold her small amount of coffee. Twice a year she bought meat, in May and for the Christmas meal.

The next family consists of a husband, 54, wife, 28, and daughter, 11. The *kibanja* area, cultivated traditionally, is 0.72 ha. In the survey year they had no *omusiri*, but did have a tiny plot of sweet potatoes on the outskirt of the *kibanja*, and two cows, which the husband spent most of his time looking after. Total work in the *kibanja* was 1 239 hours; the wife contributed 642 hours and friends and visitors 135 hours. The husband worked 462 hours in the *kibanja*. Total yearly expenditure was 275/05 shs. Farmer 15:

	Purchases	shs	Monthly total
January	Fish	2/10	
	Spices	–/60	
	Sweet potatoes	–/20	
	Maize flour	1/10	
	Cigarettes	2/–	
	Kerosene	1/40	
	Rel. offerings	–/40	7/90
February	Meat	1/–	
	Fish	2/–	
	Spices	–/20	
	Salt	–/70	
	Sugar	–/80	
	Beer	4/–	
	Cigarettes	1/90	
	Chewing coffee	–/30	
	Soap	1/40	
	Househ. equip.	1/–	
	Kerosene	2/60	
	Matches	–/10	61/40
	Clothes	42/–	
	Transport	3/–	
	Medicine	–/20	
	Cattledip	–/20	61/40
March	Fish	–/80	
	Salt	–/20	
	Cooking oil	–/20	
	Beer	2/–	
	Cigarettes	2/30	
	Soap	1/–	
	Househ. equip.	1/–	
	Kerosene	2/70	
	Cattledip	–/80	
	Hired labour	15/–	
	Other expenses	25/–	
April	Fish	5/50	
	Spices	–/20	
	Salt	1/40	
	Cooking oil	–/40	
	Cigarettes	2/60	
	Chewing coffee	3/–	
	Soap	–/40	
	Kerosene	1/10	
	Rel. offerings	–/30	
	Cattledip	1/–	13/30
May	Salt	1/30	
	Cooking oil	–/30	
	Cigarettes	2/30	
	Soap	1/20	
	Kerosene	1/05	
	Cattledip	–/60	6/75

	Purchases	shs	Monthly total
June	Meat	1/50	
	Cooking oil	–/30	
	Cigarettes	–/30	
	Kerosene	–/50	
	Clothes	20/–	
	Transport	17/50	
	Rel. offerings	–/10	
	Cattledip	–/70	40/90
July	Meat	3/–	
	Salt	–/40	
	Other food	2/–	
	Cigarettes	–/90	
	Kerosene	1/20	
	Society fee	50/–	
	Cattledip	1/–	58/50
August	Meat	1/50	
	Cigarettes	–/20	
	Househ. equip.	2/50	
	Kerosene	–/30	
	Transport	2/–	
	Cattledip	10/60	17/10
September	Fish	1/–	
	Salt	–/60	
	Kerosene	–/80	2/40
October	Fish	–/50	
	Salt	–/20	
	Kerosene	1/30	2/–
November	Salt	–/60	
	Beer	2/–	
	Cigarettes	–/05	
	Chewing coffee	–/60	
	Kerosene	2/65	
	Medicine	–/60	6/50
December	Salt	–/20	
	Beer	5/–	
	Cigarettes	–/40	
	Soap	–/80	
	Kerosene	–/90	7/30

The first half of the year he still had some money from the previous year's coffee and he received his second payment in February. In the first half of the year he could still afford some major expenses for clothes and even labour for pruning his bananas, as he was not well. When he had paid his society fee in July he kept his expenses very low the rest of the year. He received 196/– shs for his coffee that year. Nearly every month he and his family had a single meal with fish or meat.

A full-time farmer. Average type

The family consists of husband, 45, wife, 35, two sons, 17 and 10, and one daughter, 9. The *kibanja* of 1.13 ha is mainly in the traditional style. The wife had at the beginning of the year 0.06 ha *omusiri* with groundnuts and beans, and at the end of the year she hoed up two plots for groundnuts (0.23 ha and 0.06 ha, respectively). The total expenditure was 834/55 shs in 1969. In the following summary only the monthly totals are listed and for each month the expenditures larger than 5/– shs are noted. Farmer 19:

Months	Total monthly expenditure	Purchases of more than 5/– shs per month. Items
January	41/60	Meat, fish, beer, cigarettes, grass
February	52/30	Meat, fish, cigarettes, clothes
March	19/30	Cigarettes
April	17/75	Cigarettes
May	14/30	Cigarettes
June	469/50	Meat, fish, maize flour, beer, cigarettes, radio (250/–), clothes, hospital, school fees and hired labour
July	81/20	Meat, fish, maize flour, beer, cigarettes, clothes, medicine and hired labour
August	32/–	Fish, beer, cigarettes
September	26/80	Meat, cigarettes
October	34/40	Meat, beer, cigarettes
November	17/40	Cigarettes
December	28/–	Beer, cigarettes

Apart from his cigarette consumption, on which he regularly spent 10/– to 12/– shs per month, his expenditure pattern is fairly typical. The months he sold his coffee, he managed to cover more than half of his total expenditure. In June he bought a radio which he later sold again when he was short of money. Clothes and hospital treatment were some other major expenses in the two months June and August. The hired labour was used for cutting grass mulch for the *kibanja*. An interesting feature is his regular expenses for meat and fish.

A well-off part-time farmer

The last case study consisted of a family of 10 members: husband, 42, wife, 38, sons, 17, 14, 5 and 3, and daughters, 15, 12, 9 and 8. The *kibanja* consisted of 15 different pieces, with 0.46 ha in the new style and 1.04 ha in the traditional mixture. The total labour input in 1969 was 4 546 hours, of which 346 hours were done by employed labourers. The husband's share of the working hours was 406 hours. The wife had a small plot of 0.04 ha of *omusiri* with groundnuts and beans. This farmer was also a business man, buying beans and bananas from other farmers in the villages and selling

108

them to traders or to the nearby FTC. His total expenditure was 1 339/95 shs in 1969. His total expenditure per month is listed below and for each month purchases of more than 10/– shs are noted. Farmer 21:

Months	Total monthly expenditure	Purchases of more than 10/– shs per month. Items
January	78/75	Maize flour, beer, household equip.
February	58/35	Hired labour
March	82/–	Transport, hospital
April	27/95	Hired labour
May	109/80	Clothes, grass, hired labour
June	221/55	Grass, hired labour
July	64/55	Hospital, grass
August	141/20	Meat, manure (FYM), hired labour
September	97/25	Meat, household equip., clothes
October	79/55	Fish, clothes, bicycle, housebuilding
November	152/–	Fish, household equip., clothes, school fees, housebuilding, grass
December	227/–	Household equip., clothes, social contributions, hired labour

Expenditure	(shs)
December 1969	
Meat	6/–
Fish	6/–
Vegetables	1/–
Salt	3/90
Sugar	3/–
Bread	–/40
Rice	1/–
Flour	1/–
Eggs	1/05
Beer	5/50
Tea	1/75
Cigarettes	1/–
Personal art.	1/20
Soap	3/70
Paper	–/20
Household equip.	47/–
Clothes	91/50
Transport	4/50
Medicine	1/70
Social contr.	12/60
Grass	3/–
Hired labour	30/–
Total	227/–
Main groups in 1969	
Food	214/40
Drink	68/70
Cigarettes	9/30
Personal art., soap	25/60

Household equip., keros.	143/75
Clothes	151/05
Bicycle	23/75
Transport	36/50
Hospital, medicine	60/–
School fee	20/–
Social contributions	29/35
Religious offerings	–/95
Investments in house and land	556/80
Total	1 339/95

Besides the major expenses he had all the usual small expenses, as may be illustrated by going through a single month, e.g., December.

Summary

The household budget material gave as a pilot study quite an interesting understanding of the different possibilities and the different economic levels in a rural area. The scale of economics went from subsistence to well-off farmers, but the truly rich farmers were omitted from the study, as it was too difficult to get reliable data from them.

The main feature is that the cash crop coffee and the money economy deriving from this crop has developed the beginning of a specialized economy with some service facilities. The farmers are able to supplement their main food, bananas, with valuable proteins, although still on a modest scale.

The money economy has given rise to the purchase of certain items which were formerly produced by the family itself, such as labour, grass, manure, certain food items, household equipment and housing facilities. In particular, the iron sheets for the corrugated roof have become a general status symbol. The money economy has also opened up possibilities for the business-minded person: the middleman in trading and the moneylender. Economic transactions such as pledge and mortgage and the buying and selling of land are now common.

One can conclude that the money economy has created a mini-capitalistic society with a class formation of small-scale part-time farmers and full-time farmers at very different economic levels. The characteristic feature of this society is that specialization has not gone so far. It is still basically a rural society.

Chapter 9. The Social and Political Aspects of the Farming System

The Second Five-Year Plan of Tanzania gives top priority to rural development along with the implementation of the principles of *Ujamaa Vijijini* to build socialism into the rural economic sector. Gradual movement toward an integrated rural economy will create a socialist society, which is the ultimate aim of the government.

This goal is to be achieved through a reorganization of rural and urban societies into socialist production and living. The idea is to build on the principles of the traditional extended family system, and the objectives are to farm the village land collectively.[1]

This policy is founded upon the assumption that there existed three basic principles of traditional *ujamaa* living: mutual respect, sharing of joint production and work by all (J. K. Nyerere, 1967).[2]

This ideology has major implications not only for the general organization of work to obtain greater output but especially in connection with the relationship between people, as moving towards a better standard of living in this context means moving towards human equality.

We shall therefore look at the farming system from a social point of view of human equality in relation to the main components of the farming system: annual crops, perennial crops and cattle.

Annual crops

We have described before how certain communal activities are performed in cultivating the annual food crops, e.g., women plant beans together in the *kibanja*, they plant groundnuts together and bambara nuts in the *omusiri* plots and they share the work of guarding the crops against vermin. These activities are called *ujamaa* activities in the Bukoba society, but they are not *ujamaa* activities in the new sense of the word, as they only cover particular sections of the cultivation of the annuals and no joint sharing of the production takes place. Normally, they are merely social activities and have no influence on the economy in terms of greater output. On the other hand, this mutual help is of major

social and economic importance at times of illness-caused crisis in the family production system. This mutual help assures the maintenance and production of the food crops, and the links between the members of these groups of women cut across extended family systems and clan ties and in many areas are based on neighbourhood and friendship relations.

This social co-operation also takes place when unexpected guests arrive or during major family events such as weddings and deaths. Thus, in every village in Bukoba, women have organized themselves into groups which can go into action when needed. They contribute work, but are also able to raise money if necessary, e.g., for payment of hospital treatment.

The efficiency of the group depends partly on its small size of no more than 25 women and partly on the leader, who is the first among equals. The leader will call upon the group for work and will, e.g., negotiate with the holder of a certain piece of *rweya* for the cultivation of the *omusiri* crops. She will also decide which area of the fallow grassland is fit for cultivation of the *omusiri* crops. Before independence the chiefs and subchiefs of some parts of the District where bambara nuts are grown had a specially appointed man in charge of the *omusiri* cultivation. This man was called *omwarambwa* and he allocated the women the area to cultivate on the *rweya* every year and pointed out a special plot to be cultivated communally for the benefit of the chief. The cultivation started with the worshipping of the god called *Nyakalembe*, who was a fertility god. The *omusiri* plots are often located side by side on the grass-slopes and give the appearance of one large field; this is partly a relic from the time of the chiefs and partly because of the social satisfaction of working near each other.

The worshipping of *Nyakalembe* is now only practised by a few old women; the Roman Catholics, who have always been much more pragmatic than the Lutherans, have managed to transfer the worship from *Nyakalembe* to the Virgin Mary. Thus, today the farm women bring their beans and bambara nuts to the Catholic Church and have them blessed before planting. In this way the role of religion in everyday life is maintained.

We mention this last example to stress the importance of understanding the cultural background of the society when trying to change it, especially when the main idea of the new transformation of the rural areas along the lines of *ujamaa* is to use persuasion and not force.

The above-mentioned social groups of women are not official or registered. They are spontaneous and flexible and their influence is limited to small geographical areas. They help to maintain a certain standard of living, but the groups do not play any role in rural development, although some of their leaders also will be active in official women's associations such as UWT (*Umoja wa Wanawake wa Tanzania*) and *Bethania* (The Women's Association within the Lutheran Church). They could, however, play an important role if they were recognized as growth poles for *ujamaa* transformation, but only in co-operation with their menfolk.

The role of the woman in agricultural development

There is a striking misconception of the role of the woman in the Bukoba farming system. Although she does most of the work with the annual crops (as we have shown, she may even devote more time to the annual crops than to the *kibanja* cultivation), she is not recognized as a farmer, and the crops on which she spends her time have, until the *ujamaa* villages came into being, not been given much attention by either the Extension Service or the Farmers' Training Centre. When has a group of women farmers been offered a course at the FTC on improved cultivation of annual crops? This shows that there exists a close relationship between social status and crops in the Bukoba farming system. While the woman does not gain recognition for her labour-demanding work with annual crops, her role in relation to the main perennial food crop, the cooking bananas (*ebitoke*), is highly recognized.

Perennial crops. Bananas and coffee

Ebitoke is the staple food in Bukoba and some of our informants have underlined the prestige attached to *ebitoke* as food. If a farmer has no *ebitoke* for food and the family must eat either sweet potatoes or cassava,

the farmer will close the door during meal hours, so that passers-by cannot see the modest food. If the farmer and his family are eating a very excellent meal of *ebitoke* with beans or bambara nuts, and perhaps even some fish or meat, however, then he will have the door open, so that everybody can see the family eating this high-standard meal.

Friedrich (1968) recognized both a horizontal and a vertical order in plant growth, related to application of manure, as seen in decreasing fertility of the soil the further one moves away from the house. Thus the bananas are usually largest and most productive near the house and diminish in size and yield with increasing distance from the house. This is also reflected in the Luhaya terms and values attached to different bananas; e.g., "Ekitoke kya Nynenju" is a special bunch for the head of the family, often produced near the house. Such a bunch cannot be given away without consultation within the family, and the wife will try to keep one for the husband's food, when he comes back from a long journey.

On the other hand, "Akatoke K'Omumpelero" is a bunch of bananas found at the edge of the *kibanja*; it is small and considered inferior and cannot be used when special guests are present or at festivals. (The authors once weighed 30 bunches of *ebitoke* collected for a wedding party. No bunch had a weight of under 60 lbs and several weighed up to 100 pounds.)

The woman as administrator of the family food and needs

The division of labour between men and women puts the men in charge of banana husbandry: the digging of holes, the manuring of the soil and the planting and maintenance of the banana plants—as certain skills are required to maintain the *kibanja* in such a way that one obtains a regular yield of bananas throughout the year. At least traditionally, the wife prepared the *kibanja* land and then told the husband how many new banana plants were needed for the household. He then had the responsibility of planting the bananas and maintaining them. It has been difficult to trace the origin of this division of labour concerning the main food crop. Some farmers told us that at the time when age-groups were still common in the Haya society, the young men went to the King's court to serve, and at the same time they learned how to build the traditional Haya house and how to maintain a banana *kibanja*.

The woman has her particular responsibility because

the husband does not know anything about how much is necessary for food, how much should be given away to fulfill social obligations and how much is needed for celebrations. The wife is fully in charge of the administration and planning of the main food crop, whereas the husband decides about the beer-bananas. Her role as the decision-maker is recognized to the extent that it is considered very impolite to go and ask a husband for a bunch of *ebitoke*, since the person in charge should be approached.

Before the introduction of the cash crop coffee, the husband was supposed to travel to find work to earn money for the payment of taxes and the purchase of clothes. The woman was in charge of the subsistence production at home. With the introduction of coffee as a cash crop intermixed with bananas, the husband remained at home, and became responsible for the cash crop. The wife nevertheless remained fully aware of how much was produced from the *kibanja* in the form of coffee. As one farmer put it, a true Muhaya with

Cutting a bunch of bananas for the daily food.

"Ekitoke kya Nynenju", a big bunch of bananas grown near the house.

peace in his house will leave the money from the coffee to his wife to take care of. She will know how much is needed for clothes, equipment, everyday necessities like salt and tea, etc. When she had decided, they will discuss what to do with any surplus which may occur.

Thus, the Haya woman has a very important role in the family life when there is *ujamaa* in the family. She has a silent power both socially and economically, even if the husband has the last word. The coffee industry boomed, however, and individualism grew in economic activities—this base of equality and mutual respect vanished in many families; especially where the husband is a part-time farmer, the wife will be ignorant of the husband's income from work outside the farm unit.

Neither the husbandry of bananas nor the husbandry of coffee has seen any kind of communal work among the men, like that found among the women. Mutual help takes place on very large farm units, but the large farmers primarily manage their *kibanja* area with the help of hired labour. Co-operation among men takes place in sectors outside the crop production, e.g., house-building, cattle-herding and hunting.

Peeling Ebitoke for a wedding party.

The implications of coffee trading

In Chapter 5 we pointed to certain exploitative features in the Bukoba economy closely linked with increasing coffee production. From Diagram 12, page 56, it can be seen that coffee prices boomed in the middle of the 1950s; such a boom has a tremendous effect on a society where the money economy is only a few generations old. The effect was heightened by the fact that the boom was followed by depressions in the early and the late 1960s. People got rich overnight, spent a lot of money and became poor again. At the same time, from 1930 onwards this was a resource for clever and business-minded people to exploit. At first this resource (the coffee production) was exploited by the private traders during the colonial days up until 1950, when the Bukoba Native Co-operative Union was registered. As Diagram 12 shows, the Union was favoured the first five years of its existence by the coffee boom and was therefore able to accumulate funds to take over the functions of the Bukoba Native Coffee Board, to set up its own Marketing Section in 1956, and to take over the Bukoba Coffee Curing Company in 1959. Farmers immediately received better prices for their coffee, partly because of the boom and partly because of the introduction of the first and final payment system.

Unfortunately, the final payment system soon gave

Preparing of the Ebitoke meal inside the hut.

rise to renewed exploitation through the so-called "Obutura" system. *Obutura* is the name for the small unripe coffee berry and is used as a term to describe the buying of coffee on other peoples' trees in advance, before the coffee has matured.

The small holder in need of money during seasons when he cannot deliver his own coffee to the Society goes to a rich farmer or businessman to obtain a certain amount of money. The amount of money may be according to the estimated yield from his coffee trees. The buyer, who goes with the smallholder to inspect the trees, will normally underestimate the yield. He pays the smallholder an amount equal to or slightly higher than the first payment of the estimated yield, and then puts the final payment into his own pocket as a "reward" for his service. Thus, the smallholder is cheated in that he does not get the full value of the first payment of his crop and furthermore he loses his final payment. He is kept in a vicious circle.

One side effect of the *obutura* system is the bad quality of the coffee because of the methods of picking, as the buyer will be so eager to obtain all the coffee quickly that his pickers will strip off all the coffee beans (ripe and unripe) and they may even damage the trees. (This was also observed by Mr. Kamugisha in his 1970 report).[3] The moneylender fears that the smallholder will pick some of the coffee on the sly.

Many smallholders pick their coffee themselves but sell the product directly (fresh or dried) to the coffee traders for the first payment. These people may be old farmers with no one to help them with the drying and processing and transport to the Society, or they may be people who merely want to satisfy an immediate demand for, e.g., beer. It may also be necessary to sell to a trader if there is illness in the family at the time of the coffee harvest. Thus, the trader has innumerable opportunities to buy coffee and in certain cases a village may be completely dependent on one trader.

What makes the whole exploitation through trading more difficult to combat is the lack of feeling of exploitation among the smallholders. They merely look upon the *obuturu* buyer and the trader as benefactors, because they have no other way of obtaining money at any time of the year, when they are in need.

Loans with high interest and loss of kibanja

The same person is often both moneylender and coffee trader. The normal practice is that you pay back double the amount which you have borrowed. If you pay back over 6 months, this means an interest rate of 200 per cent. Nevertheless, there are just as many types of agreement as there are individual loan transactions. Often a short-term agreement is to pay back the same amount as borrowed. Then if the borrower fails to repay at the agreed date, the loan is prolonged a short period, but this time with the high interest rate of 200 per cent.

Very unfortunately, the loan transactions are often combined with the mortgaging of the *kibanja*. This means that the borrower may eventually lose his farm unit or part of it, if he is unable to repay his loan. This has strengthened the move towards greater individualism in land tenure and it has been supported by the colonial legal system. If the clan members can afford it, they may collect the necessary money and pay the debt in order to redeem the land; otherwise, the *kibanja* will be legally transferred to the lender. The clan seems to have lost any claim on the land in the future.

In the case where the clan has allowed a member to sell a piece of *kibanja* held under clan ownership, the buyer will attempt to have a document written with a higher price than that which he really paid. For example, the document may read: "Mr. N. N. has sold this piece of *kibanja*, located at y and worth 3 000 Shs, to Mr. X. X. The payment has been fulfilled according to the agreement," although the real payment was, e.g., 1 500 Shs. The trick played here diminishes the possibility of the clan raising the money and reclaiming the land, but the matter is extremely complicated and gives rise to innumerable court cases. The authors have in several cases of surveying given up the attempt to map plots of *kibanja*, because the right of ownership was disputed among various people.

Coffee marketing and class formation

The rapid development of the cash economy in Bukoba District during 40 years of colonial rule (the real expansion of coffee cultivation can be dated back to around 1920; see Diagram 12) inevitably led to the development of all kinds of corruption at all levels in the marketing of the crop. There is nothing strange about this, considering that the policy of the colonial administration was a policy of development through business, based on Western European principles. At no time before independence was there any real attempt to achieve a fair distribution of resources or income among the Bahaya smallholders, whereas the rich farmers were constantly encouraged.

It must be emphasized that from the very start of the BCU Ltd., the administration of the Union has constantly been fighting the corruption which crops up from time to time in the primary societies. Much training in running the primary societies and main office has been given, funds have been accumulated for the benefit of the farmers (e.g., the education fund) and all the activities of the BCU and its affiliated societies have been carried out within a democratic institutional framework. Nevertheless the Union has failed to teach its member what active democracy means, so there has been a great amount of authoritative execution of power, while nepotism has played a major role in the selection of primary committee members and in the grading of the coffee at the local level.

This is due to the capitalist-oriented management of the Union, which has developed into an economic bureaucracy. Thus far, the bureaucratic attitudes of the Union with all its favouritism have influenced officials at a lower level.

While it is far more impressive to regard what BCU has achieved in 20 years in the way of improvements for the marketing of their members' crops, it is also important to the stratification of Bukoba rural society and how these factors have favoured the exploitative forces in the community.

How can smuggling and excessive deliveries take place?

Coffee smuggling has been a problem during the last ten years. From 1961 to 1967 the smuggling was out of Bukoba District to Uganda, as prices were better in Uganda. From 1967 onwards smugglers have brought low-quality *Robusta* coffee from Uganda into Bukoba. Some of the coffee which enters West Lake Region through Ngara District may come from Uganda. It is difficult to assess the amount of coffee smuggled, although it was estimated to be in the range of 2 000 tons in 1967/68. The major smugglers (who are well known to the public) bring the coffee in by lorries; if the police were effective, this could fairly easily be stopped, although some difficulties would be encountered when the smugglers are licensed transporters transporting coffee from the primary societies to Bukoba. It is far more difficult to control coffee coming into the District in small quantities by boat.

There are only a few major smugglers, but there are many traders who deliver far more coffee than they are able to produce from their own *kibanja*. According to the rules of primary society membership, every member of a society must cultivate within the geographical area demarcated for delivery to that society. The smugglers and the traders often buy a tiny piece of *kibanja* in the areas of different primary societies and in that way spread their deliveries over more than one society. Nevertheless, they just as frequently do not bother to legitimize their selling in this way, being content to bribe the committee members to receive the delivery. Each new member of a primary society is required to have his membership confirmed at a general meeting and no member is allowed without the authority of the society to "deliver, sell, give or otherwise dispose of any coffee and Maganda to any firm, person or body of persons other than the society", yet there seem to be no rules saying that members must deliver coffee according to their own acreage. About 75 per cent of all farmers are estimated to be members of primary societies. Many members register their wife or sons as members, and if they only use the first or the second name of the person, only the secretary or the committee members will be able to trace their relationship, and these members will be able to deliver, e.g., a large *obutura* harvest in the names of perhaps 5 to 10 different persons. The fact that the traders and the moneylenders use this delivery technique does not mean that they are trying to conceal a crime; it is merely an old trick to hide their real income and to make it more difficult for the tax-collectors. This was certainly the primary reason until 1969, when personal taxation was abolished by the Tanzanian Government, and it was a quite understandable reaction during the colonial regime, when the tax-collectors represented the Colonial Government.

Today, in 1971, the large farmers and traders continue to use the same delivery technique, but now primarily because they fear the policy of the Nation. For the same reason they are afraid to deposit their surplus income in the bank.

Obviously the BCU has never been concerned about whether or not farmers deliver only the coffee they have grown on their own farm units, and no rules are laid down in the Co-operative Society Act to deal with this problem. Therefore, until 1967, with the publication of the *Arusha Declaration* and *Socialism and Rural Development* and, in 1971, *The Dar Declaration*, the BCU was mainly concerned about running their marketing organization at maximum efficiency as a business. They also gave concern to improving the husbandry of coffee and bananas through their extension service and loan policy and they sponsored education by giving funds for school fees and scholarships to their members. Everything was done to the best of the ability of the Union leaders in co-operation with the civil servants, both parts acting according to the political and religious standards which they had been taught by the English civil servants and teachers and the German and Scandinavian missionaries. This superimposing of the cultural, religious and business institutions of the Western world broke down what existed of traditional *ujamaa* and favoured individualism and class formation in rural society.

Göran Hydén says in his West Lake Study (1969): "Unequal distribution of wealth, status and power was accepted as a divine rule in traditional Buhaya. The inequality was less visible in Karagwe where Bahima and Bairu lived physically more excluded from each other than in the eastern part."

If this is true, the breakdown of the sovereignty of the kings or chiefs merely meant a transfer of the wealth and power to the new elite, as we have described on pages 45–46. The masses remained passive, and although the peasant society as a whole benefited from the general progress of a cash economy and increasing education, their development did not keep pace with the rapid economic development of the elite.

The gap between the rich and poor increased steadily, and at the same time there became instilled in the Haya world the doctrine that there were only two roads to progress—business or education, or ideally a combination of the two. Agricultural work lost prestige unless it could be performed by using other people's labour.

A large, well-maintained *kibanja* remained the status symbol and the objective of the Bahaya, but it was generally accepted and shown by everyday experience that money was a necessary prerequisite for a farmer to really prosper. To this rural society, with what may be a slight, growing awareness of being exploited, but still with a general tendency to accept inequality as the *modus vivendi* came the ideology of the Arusha Declaration in early 1968 and the concept of *ujamaa* in early 1969.

Notes

1. *Tanzania Second Five-Year Plan,* Government Printer, Dar Es Salaam, 1969, page 26.

2. Julius K. Nyerere, *Socialism and Rural Development,* Government Printer, Dar Es Salaam, 1967, page 3.

3. T. A. Kamugisha, *Coffee Production, Processing and Marketing.—In Connection with the Improvement of Quality in Bukoba District West Lake Region of Tanzania,* Faculty of Agriculture, Makerere, University College, Kampala, Uganda, 1970, page 6.

APPENDIX 1

Check 10/6 -69 and 1/2 -70

Farmer ....N.N.....................
Village ....N.N.....................
Family members: .....5..............
1. Husband ......65..................
2. Wife ....56.................
3. Children ...b.19(empl) d.17 d.8 1)
4. Other ......st.1..................
House built: 1958

Date .....11/12 -68................
Sub-division .....N.N................
Water Supply .....XX.................
Cattle: Calves ....-..........
        Heifers ....-..........
        Cows ....-..........
        Bulls ....-..........

Sheep: -   Goats: -

        Hens 2

plot.	Land use	crops planted	c-trees bananas	tenure	area m²
1.	Kibanja trad. Interplanted beans, maize, yam pumkin		Ba. 871 Ar. 184 Ro. 66	Inherited from father	5472
2.	House. Rough soil walls, corrugated roof, separate kitchen, grass roof, court-yard, long entrance			"	556
3.	Kibanja modern. Bananas, beans, maize, casava. Few arabica not yet uprooted	Jan 1967	Ba. 51 Ar. 6	"	676
4.	Ekishambu. 10/6 -69 cleared holes for bananas. Modern	Aug 1969	Ba. 48	"	652
5.	Maize. 10/6 planted bananas. Modern	May 1969	Ba. 9	"	236
6.	Kibanja trad. Interplanted with beans and maize		Ba. 138 Ar. 37 Ro. 3	Bought 200/= 1963	752
7.	Ekishambu, formerly part of plot 6				164
8.	Omusiri: Groundnuts, beans, cassava, sweet potatoes. 10/6 cassava. sw. pot.	1968/69 Dec/Jan		Other peoples' land	808
9.	Ekishambu			From father	372
10.	Omusiri: Sweet potatoes 1/2 -70 harvested	March 1969		Other peoples' land	120
11.	Omusiri: Groundnuts, beans, maize, sweet potatoes, cassava	1969/70 Dec/Jan		Government land	1384

1) b=boy d=daughter st=standard empl=employed

Appendix 2

Tarehe ___9/6 -69___   Jina la Mkulima **N.N.**   Jina la muulizaji **N.N.**

Vatu wanaofanya	1	2	3	4	5	6	7	8	9	10	11	12	1	Jumla
Festo	Pauzi		Kulima wa Sembe No. I		Chakula		Pauzi			Kutembea		Pauzi		
Astiria	"	Kupalilia No. I		Kupika	"		"		Kupalilia kwa Deo MSHIRIKA			Kupika		
			hoeing		Food					walk around				
			weeding	cooking					weeding			cooking		

APPENDIX 3

Mapato	Matumizi	Chakula Kinachotumika kila siku	Namba za Sehemu za Shamba
		Chakula cha mchana	
	Fish 2/-	Mukungu wa Ndizi	
	Onions -/20	lbs. 16	No. 7
	Coffee -/30		
		1 bunch bananas	
		lbs. 16	No. 7
		Chakula cha jioni	
		Ndizi	
		Viazi Vikuu	
		Bananas	
		Potatoes	
		Kama kuna mazao mengine yaliyovunwa yaandike hapa	Namba za Sehemu za Shamba
		Coffee Arabica	
		1 Debe	No. 6
		Took 1 bunch of bananas lbs. 20 for Mr. Daudi	No. 6

Appendix 4

Extract from house-hold budget book

Daftari ya fedha taslimu   Mwezi ....August....   Mwaka ....1969....

Siku	Income Mapato	Shs.	Ce	Siku	Expenditure Matumizi	Shs.	Ce
1/8	Kuuza ndizi	10		1/8	Sigara		25
11/8	Sold bananas	3	50		Pombe	1	75
12/8	Sold bananas	4			Bicycle repair		50
14/8	Sold bananas	2		2/8	Fish	1	50
18/8	Kuuza kahawa (coffee)	36			Coffee chewing		10
22/8	Building work	5			Sweets		05
31/8	Selling Pombe	16	20		Oil for the lamp		25
					Pombe	1	20
					Soap		50
				3/8	Cigarettes		50
					Pombe	1	65
					Salt		20
					etc.		

Appendix 5

No.	Item	J	F	M	A	M	J	J	A	S	O	N	D	Number of purchases per year	Yearly expenditure Shs	
1	Meat							1.50	2.50					2	4.00	
2	Fish			1.80	2.40	4.40	1.40	1.50	7.20	2.00	10.60	0.50	1.60	22	33.40	
3	Banana (eating)	3.00			17.90	15.50	5.10	11.00		5.00	4.80	23.20	10.20	28	95.70	
4	Banana (pombe)															
5	Vegetables		0.20								0.20			2	0.40	
6	Onions											1.00	0.25	2	1.25	
7	Spices (mainly curry powder)		0.20	0.20	0.40		0.10	0.10	0.40	0.10	0.10	0.10	0.50	15	2.20	
8	Salt	0.50	0.40	0.90	1.20	2.30	0.60	2.10	1.50	1.60	0.60	1.40	1.50	30	14.60	
9	Sugar	0.40		1.00	0.75	2.25	1.90	0.75						10	7.05	
10	Fruit	1.30	1.35	1.60	1.00	1.45	0.20	0.20	1.10	0.25	0.20		2.05	34	12.70	
11	Bread & cakes	0.50		3.20	0.50			0.40	0.40	3.20	0.60			16	8.80	
12	Cassava		1.00	1.00	0.50	8.20	0.50	5.60	1.20	3.00	3.80	0.90	0.50	26	26.20	
13	Potatoes		1.80	0.80	0.50	1.30			1.00					6	5.40	
14	Rice		0.60											1	0.60	
15	Maize		1.50	0.50										4	2.00	
16	Maize flour		2.00	1.65		2.00	2.00	0.50						8	8.15	
17	Other flour															
18	Beans										1.20			2	1.20	
19	Groundnuts, bambara n.								0.50	0.30				2	0.80	
20	Cooking oil				0.80		0.30					0.20	0.50	6	1.80	
21	Eggs															
22	Millet															
23	Meals outside h.			0.60		0.50								2	1.10	
24	Other food												0.20	1	0.20	227.55
25	Local beer															
26	Beer															
27	Milk			1.00										1	1.00	
28	Tea (coffee)			1.20	0.40		0.40							4	2.00	
29	Banana juice															3.00
30	Cigarettes, snuff, tobacco															
31	Sweets	0.70	0.35	0.30	0.30		0.50	0.55	0.80	0.45	1.20	0.95	0.60	34	6.70	
32	Chewing coffee		0.40	0.55				1.10	0.20					8	1.25	7.95
33	Personal articles							1.00						1	1.00	
34	Soap	4.30	0.40	2.20	0.50	2.35	3.10	3.00	3.00	4.50	8.00	0.50	1.60	36	33.45	
35	Paper, books etc.			3.80	1.10			0.30	0.10		0.70		1.40	9	7.40	41.85
36	Household equipm.				1.80		4.35	4.05	5.00	3.00				16	18.20	
37	Furniture															
38	Firewood	1.50		5.00		0.30		2.00						4	8.80	
39	Kerosene	2.80		0.70	2.55	2.25	0.70	6.60		1.65	2.20		0.70	21	20.15	
40	Matches, stones f. light.			0.20	0.10		0.10			1.00				5	1.40	48.55
41	Clothes, shoes			20.50		1.50	5.00	13.00	55.50		0.15		3.50	12	99.15	
42	Bicycle		5.90	0.50	5.00	15.20		4.00	3.30	15.00				13	48.90	
43	Transport			7.20						1.50				2	8.70	
44	Medicine, hospital fees	5.00		0.50	24.00			4.50	3.00	7.00	1.50	5.50	5.00	12	56.00	
45	School fees							25.00						1	25.00	
46	Society fees, tax								50.00		6.00			2	56.00	
47	Social contributions	13.20	0.10	7.05	6.10	6.00	11.40	2.00	15.50	6.25	2.30	6.90	2.55	58	79.00	
48	Religious offerings									24.60				2	24.60	
49	Court cases															397.35
50	Housebuilding, repair															
51	Tools			2.00	4.30									2	6.30	
52	Manure															
53	Grass															
54	Cattle dipping															
55	Hired labour				2.00	12.50		26.00						3	39.50	
56	Other expenses				0.50									1	0.50	
57	Carpentry equipm.	5.50	5.50	15.00		9.75		4.30	24.00	4.40	14.65			30	83.10	129.40
	TOTAL	38.70	21.70	80.95	73.30	89.05	37.25	95.45	200.85	46.20	34.20	46.35	32.65		855.65	

Monthly expenditure 1969

Bibliography

Allan, W. (1965) *The African Husbandman,* London, Oliver and Boyd.

Anderson, B. (1963) Soils of Tanganyika, Ministry of Agriculture Bulletin no. 16, Dar Es Salaam.

Bakula, B. B. (1971) "The Effect of Traditionalism on Rural Development: The Orumunasi Ujamaa Village, Bukoba", in J. H. Proctor (ed.) *Building Ujamaa Villages in Tanzania.* Tanzanian Publishing House, Dar Es Salaam.

Berry, L. and E. (1969) *Land Use in Tanzania by Districts,* Research Notes no. 6. BRALUP,[1] Dar Es Salaam.

Boesen, J. (1972) *Development and Class Structure in a Smallholder Society and the Potential of Ujamaa,* I.D.R. Papers A.72.16, Copenhagen and BRALUP, Dar Es Salaam.

Boesen, J. (1973) *Stagnating Agriculture and the Distorted Structure of a Coffee Exporting Region in Tanzania.* I.D.R. Papers B.73.6, Institute for Development Research, Copenhagen.

Boesen, J. and Moody, T. and Storgaard, B. (1972) *Development Problems and a Proposed Strategy for Development Planning in West Lake Region,* I.D.R. Project Papers, West Lake, D. 72.5 (Restricted), Institute for Development Research, Copenhagen and BRALUP, Dar Es Salaam.

Bukoba Cooperative Union, *Report* (1965/66 and 1967/68).

Bukoba Native Co-operative Union Ltd., *Report for the years 1961-64.*

Cliffe, L. (1970) *The Policy of Ujamaa Vijijini and the Class Struggle in Tanzania,* Seminar Paper, Leiden, Dec. 1970.

Collinson, M. P. (1963, 64, 65) *Farm Management Surveys 2-4,* Western Agricultural Research Centre, Ukiriguru, Tanzania.

Conyers, D. (1971) *Agro—Economic Zones of West Lake Region,* Research Report no. 28, BRALUP, Dar Es Salaam.

Cory, H. and Hartnoll, M. M. (1945) *Customary Law of the Haya Tribe,* published for International African institute by P. Lund, London.

Friedrich, Karl-Heinz (1968) "Coffee–Banana Holdings at Bukoba", in H. Ruthenberg (ed.), *Smallholder Farming and Smallholder Development in Tanzania,* I.F.O. no. 24, London, C. Hurst.

Gillman (1936) *Rweya Pasture,* Notes, Maruku District Book.

Haarer, A. E. (1962) *Modern Coffee Production,* London, L. Hill.

Haarer, A. E. (1964) *Modern Banana Production,* London, L. Hill.

Harvey, C. (1937) *Rweya Land Cultivation,* Notes, Maruku District Book, Tanzania.

Hydén, G. (1969) *Political Development in Rural Tanzania, A West Lake Study,* East African Publishing House, Nairobi.

Ishengoma, J. S. (1956) *Rweya Land Cultivation,* Maruku District Book.

James, R. W. (1971) *Land Tenure and Policy in Tanzania,* East African Litterature Bureau, Dar Es Salaam.

Jensen, S. B. and Jumanne, M. (1968) *District Data 1967,* Ministry of Economic Affairs and Development Planning, Dar Es Salaam.

Jervis, T. S. (1939) *A History of Robusta Coffee in Bukoba.* Tanganyika Notes and Records, no. 8, Dar Es Salaam.

Kamugisha, T. A. (1970) *Coffee Production, Processing and Marketing. In Connection with the Improvement of Quality in Bukoba District, West Lake Region of Tanzania,* Faculty of Agriculture, Makerere, University College, Kampala.

Kibira, J. M. (1964) *A Study of Christianity Among the Bahaya Tribe: West Lake Region, Tanganyika,* Unpublished S.T.M. Thesis, Boston University School of Theology.

Kinyondo, S. R. (1971) *The Building of Socialism in Tanzania, Katoma Traditional Village: A Case Study of Problems and Possibilities of Transforming a Traditional Village into an Ujamaa Village,* Political Science—Paper 7 (a) Dissertation, University of Dar Es Salaam.

Kostrowicki, J. (1966) *Principles, Basic Notions and Criteria of Agricultural Typology,* International Geographical Union.

McMaster, D. (1960) *Change of Regional Balance in the Bukoba District of Tanganyika,* The Geographical Review, Vol. L, no. 1.

Map Sheets, *Series Y 742, 1/50 000 Scale,* Bukoba District. Surveys and Mapping Division, Dar Es Salaam.

Mbilinyi, S. M. (1968) *Estimates of Peasant Farmers' Costs of Production: The Case of Bukoba Robusta Coffee.* Economic Research Bureau, 68 : 1, University of Dar Es Salaam.

Milne, G. (1938) *Bukoba, High and Low Fertility on a Laterised Soil,* East African Agricultural Research Station Report XIV, Amani.

Milne, G. (1938) "Essays in Applied Pedology III Bukoba—High and Low Fertility on a Laterised Soil", *East African Agricultural Journal,* Vol. 4.

Mitchell, H. W. (1963) *Results of a Coffee and Banana Interplanting Trial In Bukoba,* Tanganyika Coffee Board Research Report.

Moody, T. (1970) *A Report on Farm Economic Survey of Tea Smallholders in Bukoba District.* East African Agricultural Economies Society Conference, Dar Es Salaam.

Moody, T. (1972) *Notes on the Prospects for Class Consolidation in Bukoba.* IDR Project Papers, West Lake D.72.4, Inst. for Development Research, Copenhagen.

Moody, T. (1972) *The Bukoba Tea Scheme: Ten Years of Development,* "Mapinduzi Majani", IDR Paper, West Lake A.72.12, Inst. for Dev. Research, Copenhagen and BRALUP, Dar Es Salaam.

Moody, T. (1973) *How Studies and Policies over-estimate the Potential for Rural Populations to Develop into Agriculture from Subsistence.* Inst. for Dev. Research, Copenhagen.

Mukurasi, P. W. (1970) *The Bukoba Co-operative Union as an Instrument of Agricultural Innovation,* Political Science—Paper 7: Dissertation, University of Dar Es Salaam.

Musoke, I. K. S. (1970) *Who Holds Power in Bukoba?* TAAMULI., A Political Science Forum, Vol. 1, no. 1, University of Dar Es Salaam.

Musoke, I. K. S. (1971) "Building Socialism in Bukoba: The Establishment of Rugazi (Nyerere) Ujamaa Village", in *Building Ujamaa Villages in Tanzania,* edited by J. H. Proctor, Tanzania Publishing House. Dar Es Salaam.

Mutahaba, G. (1969) *The Importance of Peasant Consciousness for Effective Land Tenure Reform. The Problem of Abolishing Nyarubanja Land Tenure in Bukoba District.* Political Science Undergraduate Dissertation, University of Dar Es Salaam.

Møberg, J. P. (1970) *Report Concerning the Soil Profile Investigation*

[1] BRALUP=Bureau of Resource Assessment and Land Use Planning, University of Dar Es Salaam.

and Collection of Soil Samples in the West Lake Region of Tanzania, Rep. Scand. Inst. Afr. Studies, 6, Uppsala, Sweden.

Møberg, J. P. (1972) Some Soil Fertility Problems in the West Lake Region of Tanzania, Including the Effects of Different Forms of Cultivation, on the Fertility of Some Ferralsols, *East African Agricultural and Forestry Journal,* Vol. XXXVIII, no. 1.

Møberg, J. P. (1973) An edaphological and pedagogical investigation of the soils in the West Lake Region of Tanzania. University of Copenhagen, Denmark.

Ngeze, P. B. N. M. (1968) *Report on an Appraisal of the Economics of Banana Growing as Compared to Coffee and Tea in the Bukoba District,* Makerere University College, Kampala.

Nyerere, J. K. (1967) *Socialism and Rural Development,* Government Printer, Dar Es Salaam.

Nyerere, J. K. (1967) *The Arusha Declaration,* TANU, Government Printer, Dar Es Salaam.

Pitblado, J. R. (1970). *A Review of Agricultural Land Use and Land Tenure in Tanzania,* Research Notes no. 7, BRALUP, Dar Es Salaam.

Prynø, H. (1971) *Potential Land Use Classification in Connection with the Kishanda Valley Project,* Research Report no. 27, BRALUP, University of Dar Es Salaam.

Rald, J. (1969) *Land Use in a Buhaya Village,* Research Paper no. 5, BRALUP, University of Dar Es Salaam.

Rald, J. and Mutahaba, G. (1969) *Progress Report on Ujamaa Vijijini-Orumunazi, Ihangiro, Bukoba District,* Regional Office, West Lake.

Rald, J. (1970) *Ujamaa. Problems of Implementation. (Experiences from West Lake),* Research Report no. 10, BRALUP, University of Dar Es Salaam.

Reining, P. C. (1962) Haya Land Tenure: Land Holding and Tenancy. *Anthropological Quarterly,* Vol. 35. no. 2.

Reining, P. C. (1965) "Land Resources of the Haya", in D. Brokensha (ed.), *Ecology and Development in Tropical Africa,* Research Series no. 9, University of California.

Reining, P. C. (1967) *The Haya: The Agrarian System of a Sedentary People,* Ph.D. Anthropology, University of Chicago.

Reining, P. C. (1970) "Social Factors and Food Production in an East African Peasant Society: The Haya", in Peter McLoughlin (ed.), *African Food Production Systems,* John Hopkins. U. Press.

Simmonds, N. W. (1959) *A Report of all Banana Work Done at Maruku,* UPTO, 1967.

Simmonds, N. W. (1962) *The Evolution of the Bananas,* Tropical Science Series, edited by D. Rhind, Longmans.

Storgaard, B. (1972) *A Preliminary Report on Socio-Economic Patterns in an Urbanized Rural Area and the Response to Planned Development. (A Case Study from Maruku Area, Bukoba District.)* IDR Project Papers, West Lake A 72.15, Inst. for Dev. Research, Copenhagen and BRALUP, University of Dar Es Salaam.

Tanzania, Second Five-Year Plan. Gov. Printer, Dar Es Salaam.

Tothill, J. D. (1940) *Agriculture in Uganda,* Oxford University Press, London.

Trewartha, G. T. (1961) *The Earth's Problem Climates,* Madison.

Walwa, P. C. (1967) (ed.) *Mpango wa Kutekeleza Azimio la Arusha Mkoa wa Ziwa Magaridi,* Bukoba Printers.

West Lake Annual Report, (1967, 68, 69) Ministry of Agriculture.

Western Research Centre (1966) *Groundnut Cultivation in Western Tanzania,* Progress Report no. 2.